Successful Self-Publishing:
(How We Do It, and How You Can Too)

SHOSHANNA EVERS

Successful Self-Publishing:
(How We Do It, and How You Can Too)

Edited by Shoshanna Evers

Copyright Shoshanna Evers 2012, 2014
Note: Each author retains copyright on his or her own contribution.

Successful Self-Publishing: How We Do It, and How You Can Too
Edited by Shoshanna Evers

Copyright © 2012 Shoshanna Evers
Updated edition copyrighted © 2014 Shoshanna Evers
Please see Copyright Acknowledgements for individual copyright holder information for each article. Every contributor retains copyright to his or her article.
All Rights Reserved.

Cover art by Rob Sturtz www.SelfPubBookCovers.com

Electronic book publication 2012, 2014
Trade Paperback publication 2012, 2014
Any resemblance to persons living or dead or places, events or locations is coincidental.

This book is licensed for your personal enjoyment only. This book may not be resold or given away to other people. If you would like to share this book with another person, please purchase an additional copy for each reader. If you're reading this book and did not purchase it, or it was not purchased for your use only, then please return to the book store of your choice and purchase your own copy. Thank you for respecting the hard work of this author.

For a free PDF download of this ebook, visit www.SelfPubBookCovers.com.
Copyright © 2012 Author Name
All rights reserved.

DEDICATION

To every author with a story to tell, and the willingness
to work hard to make it happen.

It's time!

CONTENTS

1	Introduction	1
2	How I Make $20,000 or More a Month with my Self-Published Books	5
3	We Can	15
4	The Cover: Make it Professional!	18
5	The Business of Publishing: an interview of Shoshanna Evers by author Cara Bristol	22
6	I Did It My Way	28
7	Respect Your Readers	31
8	10, no 11 Successful Self-publishing Tips I Wish I'd Known	34
9	A Dog, A New Genre, and a Charity	38
10	A Tale of Two Novellas	41
11	The Sky Is Not Falling, or Why 99-Cent Books (Probably) Won't Take Over the World	46
12	Why I Love My Crazy Indie Life	49
13	How I Sold 17,000 books in Four Months	54
14	David Kazzie, Before & After	57
15	Twitter 101: Five Things about Twitter Authors Should Know (and Five you Don't Know)	64
16	Marketing by the eBook	70
17	The World of a Steampunk Indie	73
18	Getting Published	76

ACKNOWLEDGMENTS

Thank you to the contributors of this indie anthology, you are wonderful and I am thrilled that you've let me share your knowledge and inspiration with the writing community. Rob Sturtz of www.SelfPubBookCovers.com created our book cover, thank you for this one and the other awesome covers you've made for me over the past few years. Thank you to my readers, without you I would just be writing into the abyss. You are the reason I write!

About SelfPubBookCovers.com

Graphic designer and cover artist Rob Sturtz co-founded this website with author Shoshanna Evers in the hopes of creating a site where we could bring self-published authors together with amazing book cover artists. Being able to instantly customize our own book covers and download them will bring even more control into the self-published author's hands, and hopefully make it simple for every author to have a cover that can stand proudly next to the traditionally-published books sharing our virtual bookshelves.

We want indie authors to succeed, which is why this book is available as a free PDF download on our site. If you liked this book, please send other authors to www.SelfPubBookCovers.com to download their own free copy. Thank you!

1
INTRODUCTION
BY SHOSHANNA EVERS

Welcome! *Successful Self-Publishing: How We Do It (And How You Can Too)* is all of the advice and inspiration I've wanted to share with authors for a while now. As both an independent and traditionally published author, I can tell you from experience that there are pros and cons to both routes. Ultimately, the best thing about self-publishing is the ability to retain control over all aspects of your own book, and to make more money per sale doing so.

Numerous other successful authors have joined me to contribute their knowledge and tips on how they've achieved their goals through self-publishing. We've got specific suggestions, Do's and Don'ts, and so much energy and excitement for this new world of publishing that by the time you finish reading, you'll be ready to take the steps to put your manuscript out into the world as a published book.

I'm not against traditional publishing. I consider myself a business woman as well as an author. My business is the business of "being Shoshanna Evers." That involves much more than just writing books. More than half of my work day is spent not writing, but in publishing or promotion-related endeavors. When I heard that I could get 70% royalties based on list price if I published a book myself instead of going through one of my publishers, I made a business decision: It was time to dip my toes in the self-publishing waters. And wow, the water feels great!

We start with *USA Today* Bestseller Kallypso Masters's inspiring journey of how she quit her part-time day job making thirty grand a year (including benefits) and went on to net well over six figures as a debut indie author. She's very pro-indie, to the point that she thinks getting an agent and accepting a traditional book deal that includes her digital rights is like flushing money down the toilet.

I can see where she's coming from—after running the numbers before accepting a six-book deal with a large traditional publisher, I felt I could make more money on my own, since as JA Konrath says, 70% royalties forever is worth more than 14.9% royalties, and forever is a long time—but I wanted to try something different to see how it went. Point being, I went into it with open eyes. Whatever you do, go into a project with your eyes open and know what you're gaining and what you're losing by taking a certain route. Most important to me in any contract is that I am still able to self-publish if I sign it.

Author Gia Blue hit number twenty three on the overall Amazon Kindle Bestsellers list with a short erotic story and continues to self-pub what she calls her "smut" since she feels publishers won't touch it but…readers love it.

New York Times and *USA Today* Bestseller H.P. Mallory talks about the importance of great cover art and how to make the most of your cover to sell your books, and build your brand.

Then, author Cara Bristol interviewed me about the business of writing. In the interview I give candid answers about how I went from completely unknown (in fact, Shoshanna Evers did not exist at all, since it's my pen name) to making a living as a full-time author. It includes my tips on when—or if—to find an agent and go the traditional publishing route, or whether self-publishing is the best choice for you.

Liz Matis's book spent almost two years in editor limbo before she pulled the plug and decided to go it alone. She also talks about how she put her self-published book out as an ebook, a print book using print-on-demand, and an audio book—all with a zero to low start-up costs.

Having a high quality product that's well written, well edited, well formatted, and has a great cover are all an important part of respecting our readers, something Katriena Knights (who also writes as Elizabeth Jewell and KC Myers) discusses in her essay.

Amazon Bestselling author Heather Thurmeier gives us her top ten list of tips for successful self-publishing, plus a bonus tip. She doesn't gloss over the hard work involved or the fact that your book-baby might not sell as well as you hoped. Then again, it might…

New York Times and *USA Today* Bestselling author Jennifer Probst found a place for her story about a rescue dog by self-publishing it, and now writes a check each month with part of the book proceeds to the animal shelter where she volunteers. She found a wonderful way to contribute to charity with the gift that keeps on giving—royalties!

New York Times and *USA Today* Bestselling author Skye Warren did an experiment. She put two novellas up for sale and told no one to see what would happen. Her experiment led to some fascinating insights on self-publishing, including the importance of discoverability and word-of-mouth in the absence of marketing.

SUCCESSFUL SELF-PUBLISHING

Price points are an important facet of self-publishing, since we have the ability to be nimble with our pricing and make adjustments as needed. We can try different things to see how our books sell best and what makes the most money. I've found that when I price my books higher, I get less sales (and therefore a lower ranking on lists) but I make more money. My bestselling short story Overheated, however, is only 99 cents simply because it's too short to make it cost more, in my opinion. It outsells my other books. Jackie Barbarosa discusses the pros and cons of the 99 cent price point and whether that should be part of your marketing strategy.

Donna McDonald kept getting rejections from traditional publishers who said her books were wonderful but there was no market for an older heroine. She proved them all wrong by self-publishing and now makes a living off of her self-pub income.

I interviewed *USA Today* Bestseller Debra Holland, and she explains how good reviews and making category bestseller lists on Amazon made her sales go through the roof. She sold over 120,000 books in her first fourteen months as a debut author.

Then David Kazzie, Amazon Bestseller and creator of the viral YouTube hit "So You Want to Write a Novel" talks about how putting his book up for free brought life to lagging sales.

I've also included Valerie Bowman's Twitter primer for authors, which includes information on how to use hashtags and Triberr to maximize your follower reach. Being on Twitter is a great way to get connected to the publishing community and connect with readers.

Author K. Rowe gives her tips on marketing using free promo, including the importance of making it easy for readers to discover and get to your books via links.

So what happens if you put out a great book and it's not selling? When Heather Hiestand, (who also writes as Anh Leod) had lagging sales on one of her indie books, she took it to a review website loop and asked for honest opinions on why it wasn't selling. She changed her cover, blurb, and sale price to increase sales. One of the biggest benefits of self-publishing a book is that we can change things that don't work until they *do* work.

The last article in this book is my essay Getting Published, which breaks down all the publishing terms, what they mean, how to format your manuscript, how to write a query letter, and how to decide if you want to pursue traditional publishing, self-publishing, or as I have done, both. For this updated 2014 version, I'm thrilled to be able to add *New York Times* and *USA Today* bestselling author to my bio, as well, thanks to the self-published box set MAKE ME: Twelve Tales of Dark Desire.

If you're reading this introduction as an excerpt or sample pages, please know that you can download the book for free at www.SelfPubBookCovers.com.

We want you to be successful. This is how we do it, and how you can too.
Ready?

2
HOW I MAKE $20,000 OR MORE A MONTH WITH MY SELF-PUBLISHED BOOKS
BY KALLYPSO MASTERS

"Woo-hoo! Looks like it's gonna be another $1,000+ day! I love being a self-published author!" I e-mailed that to Shoshanna Evers in June 2012 when we were discussing this book project, which happened to be the month my self-publishing career took me to yet another new level after I made my first book free. While I don't make that much every day, I've done so more days than I can believe, especially after my fourth book was released in mid September. And I've grossed an average of more than $20,000 a month from January to November this year, which has me pinching myself to make sure this is real.

Here's how my amazing journey into self-publishing started. In March 2011, I went to a workshop/retreat to learn techniques from *The Artist's Way*, by Julia Cameron. I quickly realized (in *Artist's Way* terms) that I was in a "crazymaker" job that was also a "shadow artist" job. I was an editor working on a college catalog and in-house student publications, but what I really wanted to do for the past 25+ years was write romance novels. But I knew from watching my friends in my Romance Writers of America (RWA) chapters in Kentucky and New York over those years that writing doesn't pay the bills because you only made a tiny percentage of a book's list price. The rest was kept by your publisher and/or agent.

So, despite not having gotten even a nibble at any of the four resumes/applications for writer/editor jobs that I had sent out since January, I needed to quit to maintain my sanity and lower my stress level. I wasn't really thinking about writing for a living. I needed a job, with health benefits.

So, the Monday after the retreat, I went to work and turned in my resignations giving three-weeks' notice. My last day on the job was April 15, 2011. My Evil-Day-Job (EDJ) Independence Day.

Ever since the workshop, I'd been faithfully writing three pages in my journal—my "Morning Pages" (one of *The Artist's Way* techniques I'd learned). My creativity was so blocked that these entries are pretty much what I'd done the day before and what I planned to do this day. A diary. After a few weeks, though, I noticed that characters and plot ideas started to pop in amongst my ponderings on the day. While I continued at first to look to see what job openings came up in the area, why not write again? For decades, I'd mostly managed to write only on weekends and during vacation and holiday breaks. Rather than just sit around, might as well be productive, even if it did wind up with the eight other partial manuscripts in that tall box in the office.

After discovering erotic romances in spring 2009, I had drafted a novel in a month called *Nobody's Angel* and decided that it would be the easiest one to update and submit to Samhain Publishing (one of the biggest of the small e-book/print-on-demand publishers) and the only publisher I've ever submitted a novel manuscript to. I'd gotten a "good" rejection in spring 2009 for a novella I'd written a month before *Nobody's Angel*. While that story wasn't right, they asked to see something else, but the EDJ had intervened and I didn't write or edit a single word for almost two years.

Traditionally published authors in my online writers' loop (the Kentucky Romance Writers, KYRW, my RWA chapter) suggested I go with a publisher first, then branch out into self-publishing. (I heard that same advice at a self-publishing panel at the Romantic Times Booklovers Convention nearly a year later and had to smile at the error of the advice—in my case, at least. But I knew from watching my fellow chapter mates (most of whom had to keep their EDJs) that, by going the traditional route, I'd lose six months to two years of income IF I could get a publisher (whether New York's then Big Six, or the small e-book/POD publishers), with no guarantee of ever selling a manuscript to any of them. So two years from now, I could still be waiting for a publisher's nod and contract.

Then at the May 2009 KYRW chapter meeting, Donna Jane McDonald (also featured in this book) shared with us her first two months' experience as a self-published author. She was already seeing sales increasing and firmly believed this was the way to go if you wanted to be a full-time writer, as I did. (I remember celebrating with her a couple months later when she announced that she had used her royalties to pay her mortgage.)

I'd studied the writing craft over the previous two decades, knew how to write a story, knew the importance of hiring someone to edit it for me (not doing so is akin to a surgeon giving herself an appendectomy), and knew I could finish a manuscript (having completed two in as many months a couple years earlier). So I went home and asked my husband if he'd give me a year to make it as a full-time writer (living off our retirement savings in that year, which made my saver hubby *very* nervous). I think he agreed mainly to give me a year to regroup and recover from the last couple years of stress. He referred to my writing as "my new hobby" in the beginning, even though I was working at it from the time I got up until I went to bed.

Luckily, the bar for success set by my hubby was very low. I would only need to make about $30k a year to make up for the salary and benefits I'd lost by quitting my part-time editorial job. So, the clock began ticking in May 2011 and I became obsessed with writing (which continued for about seven months as I feverishly worked to get three books published, because Donna said that you need to get at least that many books out before you're really going to be noticed—and I was going to try to follow Donna's well-researched advice).

While the National RWA didn't recognize self-published authors as actually published (they seemed stuck on the old days and vanity-press model of self-publishing), I gained so much help from members of the local chapter, most of whom were at least doing a mix of contracts with publishers and self-publishing. (Many of us later left RWA in frustration, though, and started a group called the Kentucky Independent Writers, which is my current writer-support group.)

I learned that it's important to have a marketing piece (novella or short novel) that I either give away or sell very inexpensively to introduce readers to my style. With so many ill-prepared self-published stories on the market, readers were becoming leery of trying new authors without getting something to sample.

I immersed myself in writing *Masters at Arms* that May, which would be the Rescue Me series' introduction. I had fallen in love with BDSM erotic romances a couple years before after starting my journey in erotic romance with Cherise Sinclair's Masters of the Shadowlands series. But I didn't want to compete with Cherise's awesome "fantasy" Doms, so I decided to write about Doms who weren't perfect, screwed up regularly, were deeply wounded by life—but still were so damned sexy and lovable that the readers couldn't help but want to submit to them (or hit them upside the head on occasion).

I learned that I needed to hire an excellent cover artist who knew this specialized artform well. I tried to get Dara England, who did the covers for several writers in my group, but she wasn't accepting new clients. I couldn't afford most of the others I looked at, so I ignored my chapter mates' advice and asked Linda Lynn, a friend who is a professional graphic artist, to do them. (She said I could pay her the next year after I made some money. I loved that she had faith in me!) I have no regrets, because her covers are phenomenal, even if she isn't really into the subject matter on mine.

As I continued to write, I started looking for an editor. I didn't want to have my fellow writers to edit for me. (It may just me, but I get so much better edits from dedicated editors who don't also write.) My KYRW chapter president shared the names of two freelance editors she met at the Romantic Times Booksellers convention the month before. I chose Jeri Smith, of booksmithediting.com, because she could start sooner and her rates were extremely affordable. She was just starting her own freelance editing business after having worked with New York publishers for decades. (After editing a couple books, she learned her rates were too low, but now I can afford to pay the higher rates.)

I published *Masters at Arms* in August 2011 for 99 cents (Amazon and Barnes & Noble wouldn't allow free books at that time—I've since learned how to get around both of them, as I'll explain below, and lowered the price to free in June 2012); *Nobody's Angel* in September for $2.99 (raised that to $3.99 in June 2012); and *Nobody's Hero* (written and edited in two months) in December for $3.99. After that magical third book came out, the next month my royalties more than doubled from $5k in December to $12,200 in January. (I felt so guilty having made such an obscene amount of money that I announced I would donate everything I made over $10k in January to the Wounded Warrior Project, which I did when I received the royalties. Then my hubby lectured me on how much I was going to have to pay in quarterly taxes and reined me in a little bit, but I continue to donate as much as I can to the causes that are important to me.)

I have grossed five figures a month ever since, with March being the lowest at about $10k. (Yeah, I know—how bad is *that*?!?) That's the month I decided to hire Leagh Christensen, a personal assistant who does a phenomenal amount of work for the $500-750 a month I pay her. Within that first month, she had helped me get lots of swag ready to hand out at the 2012 RT Booklovers Convention (and attended the convention to help keep me on track); hired a Web designer and started my Web site (for which I'd purchased the domain three years earlier, but hadn't gotten any further); started an e-mail newsletter (I'd tried to start months earlier); and put together a street team of avid readers to send swag (bookmarks, trading cards, pens, etc.) to who would then "pimp" my books to their friends, family, and acquaintances everywhere they go, it seems. THEN *Fifty Shades of Grey* hit the media fan and readers who hadn't noticed erotic romances before (or the BDSM subgenre I wrote in) were suddenly looking for what to read next. So, improved April and May sales were a combination of all that publicity and some luck at having three books already published to feed the frenzy for more.

I didn't put out book four in the Rescue Me series—*Nobody's Perfect*—until September 2012 (three months after I'd said it would come out and almost nine months after the previous book). According to the advice that you need to keep putting books out so readers won't forget you didn't apply or my sales would have tanked. What saved me was making *Masters at Arms* (the introductory book) free. This book is a series of vignettes—not just prequels, but a cohesive story showing how the first three heroes in the series bonded with each other in combat and went on to start a kink club together.

Masters at Arms is basically a fun marketing piece—one great big tease. (Read it—it's free!) Most publishers wouldn't publish a prequel until after several books in the series had been successfully published, but that just seems backward to me. (My readers agree!) The book has five sections—the first three showing major turning points in the lives of three of the first heroes in the series, and showing what their feelings are about BDSM, love, duty, and more. Then in the fourth section, they come together in combat in Iraq and form a bond with each other than can never be broken. In the fifth and final vignette, we move to real-time and they've started a kink club and their own family of sorts. I also brought Karla (from section one) back to Adam as a grown woman, so she could start working on his heart. She was only 16 to his 41 years in the beginning of the book. A traditional publisher probably wouldn't have let me have a 25-year age difference between a hero and heroine, but Adam and Karla are the most popular couple in this series!

Leagh, my assistant, told me in April 2012 that "before the fourth book comes out, we're making *Masters* free." I've learned to trust her instincts about promotion and business matters, so she can Domme me all she wants. Another fortuitous event last March was when a retired Marine Master Sergeant befriended me after reading the first three books and loving them. He offered to go through *Masters* and fix a few Marine/military things to improve the story. I then hired a line editor to go over it once more and uploaded the new free version.

But Amazon wouldn't make it free at first, so I told my Street Brats team to go to Amazon and report that the book was free at Smashwords and All Romance eBooks. Well, FOUR DAYS later, Amazon made it free. Then I asked my Facebook friends (about 2,000 of them at the time) to download the new version. (Telling them it was updated got them there faster than if I'd just said it was free, because they already had the original book.) There were 54 downloads in the first hour and soon after I was averaging about 118 an hour—more than 40,000 downloads that month. That shot me onto the bestseller lists for free books (#1 in the war genre and #17-18 in Contemporary Romance, both on Amazon). Four months later, there have been more than 80,000 downloads at Amazon alone. (Not as great as some indies, but I am happy with it!)

It was a little trickier to make it free at Barnes & Noble. You need to make it free on Smashwords and have them distribute directly to Barnes & Noble. Worked like a charm!

What surprised me in June, almost immediately sales of the other two published books in the series went through the roof. They had been ranked in the low 20s on Amazon's bestselling erotica list and went as high as the top five on the list. This marketing strategy gave me, a relatively unknown author, great exposure.

I firmly believe that anyone can make a success of self-publishing if they hire the people who can make their works look as professional as possible, and you write a compelling story that pulls them in, make them think these are real people living in the real world, and keep them dying for more. (I love cliffhangers, but I always make it clear this is NOT a stand-alone series. I saw an author being lambasted in reviews for leaving readers hanging for months because she didn't label her 99-cent Black Friday special as the first in a series. Always be honest. My readers may not say they "love" cliffhangers, but they do keep coming back and asking me when the next will be released so they can find out what happened.)

Readers *love* reading series, so this is also one of the things that makes my series popular. (I have readers who tell me they've re-read the series six times already, too, and that they find new layers each time, like peeling an onion.) Many readers say they feel like these characters are a part of their own families—or that they wish they were. I also make my stories so interconnected that they cannot stand alone. To make sense of the characters and plots, readers *have* to read them in order (at least the first six books, after which I will attempt to do stand-alones). I have gotten dinged by some reviewers who didn't do that, but the majority of my reviewers all say READ THEM IN ORDER!

Not having to tie up all the loose ends for a couple in a single book has made it possible for me to be able to actually finish my books, though. I had written manuscripts for more than 20 years, but could never finish a book because I was always worried about leaving things undone or not having the perfect ending. This takes a lot of that pressure off. It also makes my romances realistic, which is rare in the genre and provide me with another niche. "Happy For Now" means the couple will need to come back later, but even my Happily Ever After endings (which, for me, means marriage or at least an engagement) requires ongoing maintenance. Couples will come back later in the series to deal with unresolved (or new) issues, either as subplots or as the main characters, which is happening with the couple in *Nobody's Angel*, who will now star in book five in the series, *Somebody's Angel*.

While my books are labeled erotica at Amazon, Smashwords, and other booksellers that don't differentiate between erotica and erotic romance, I write erotic *romances* that have kinky sex, not kinky-sex books that happen to have a simple plot that pulls together the sex scenes. I grab readers by the throat and I don't let go.

Unlike a traditionally published series with rigid word counts, I can take as long as I need to tell the story. All of my books are long. My shortest novel was the introduction, *Masters* (58,000 words). *Angel* was 116,000; *Hero* was 140,000 words; and *Perfect* came out at 171,000 (and didn't have much of a subplot, because I pulled it out to go into book five). I think I probably would make a lot more money (and sell more books) if I could write short, but I can't, so I'll just have to do what works for me. Luckily, my books are page-turners, so readers don't always notice that they're so long—or don't care.

Despite their size, I believe in keeping my book prices at no more than $3.99 each. There is debate about whether self-pubbed authors are selling themselves too cheaply, but I have a readership that is primarily military or hard-working (in and out of the home), so keeping the price down is a commitment I have made to them. Obviously, I am making a living, so there's no need to gouge my readers by charging more. But as a reader, when an e-book is priced over $4.99, I have to really know that author's work before I'll take a chance and pay that much.

As you can see by the title and content of this article, it didn't take me the full year to reach the success mark of $30,000. My husband still can't figure out how there can be hundreds of new readers every day buying my books (he is *so* not into BDSM books)—but he's starting to come around to thinking this just might be a long-term career and not a flash in the pan. (But he still makes me give him the tax money as soon as the royalties come in, because he knows I'm enjoying traveling and meeting readers way too much to have anything left later on. I went to three conferences/conventions this year and plan to attend five or six in 2013.)

So, what are my future goals for success? A lot of my traditionally published writer friends aspire to have a *New York Times* bestseller title, but I'm aware of how difficult it is for self-published authors to achieve that—although not impossible! However, that list is based on the number of books *ordered*, not on books sold, so you need an awesome distribution system. But I did make a writer's dream goal recently—the *USA Today* bestseller list. A self-publishing phenom, Bella Andre, surprised the heck out of me in late September when she Tweeted that I had made the list based on sales in the week my fourth book was released. If she or someone hadn't told me, I probably wouldn't have known! I was only on the list that one week (at #115 out of 150 of all fiction and nonfiction books sold that week), but that gives me bragging rights—and labels on my books—for life. If the *New York Times* list happens, great, but I think my primary goal is to continue make a living at this thing I love, connect with lots of readers online and in person, and have fun.

After I made the *USA Today* list, an editor for a New York megapublisher, which just merged with another mega-publisher, asked if I'd consider going traditional with the series. I told her I might consider something with the print, international, foreign translations, and audiobooks, but she said they don't offer new clients contracts without the digital rights, so that was the end of that. It may take me longer to make all those things happen, but I do have print versions in the works, and plan to publish the first four in December 2012.)

What do I aspire to next? Someday I want to win the award from readers that I am the most accessible author. I share everything on my Facebook timeline and in my groups! They know how the writing is coming, which Dom I want to string up by the balls on any given day, and what is happening in my personal life. When my first grandchild was born in September, I was surprised to go to the mailbox and find handmade gifts from two of my readers. And my sister's ongoing battle with cancer has been an ongoing concern for my readers, as well, with them often asking for updates.

So my best advice is write well and engage with readers! Simple!

I've tried placing a couple paid ads at online book blogger and bookseller sites with lackluster results, but word of mouth is the best advertising one can have—and my readers (both those on the Kallypso's Street Brats team and those I call my Masters Brats) like to "pimp" my books everywhere! One of the highlights of my week is checking in with my Brats group on Facebook to read their book-pimping stories. They've told bosses and coworkers, patients, people at the grocery or craft store, mothers volunteering at their kid's book fair at school, even mothers trick-or-treating at their door with kids on Halloween night. Heck, the other day, one even pimped me at her Bible Study after someone brought up that she was reading *Fifty Shades*. About half the women in the group had read *Fifty Shades* and were looking for more. (I have one reader who works as a cashier and she said every time someone comes through her line with *Fifty Shades*, she gives them my name as something to read after they're finished.) My readers are *that* devoted to this series and want to hook everyone they know on it. Now they tell me their friends are pimping to their friends—and the ripples continue to spread.

Start up a Facebook group (or one at Yahoo or wherever you'd like) so your street team can discuss their plans and pimping stories. I often ask them for help, too. It's like having my own book-pimping army! I hope that by the time I meet some more of them at conventions, I will have some nice gifts for them. And I'll send them buttons to wear so that anyone who comes up to me at a convention wearing my button will get a gift! I'm thinking tote bags, which are always useful at book conventions (and one size fits all!).

Facebook continues to be my primary social networking platform. I started there in May 2009 and had 625 friends when my first book came out (all but about 200 of them people who sent me friend requests after hearing about me from their friends). I now have more than 3,200 friends on my timeline account (plus another 300+ subscribers) and more than 2,000 "likes" on my Facebook Author Page (only 900 of them on both lists). I have about 3,000 newsletter subscribers, many of them probably also on Facebook.

It's also nice to give readers a place where they can discuss your books without worrying about spoilers. (I hate having spoilers in reviews or on my Facebook timeline.) This fall, my assistant started the Rescue Me Series Open Discussion group on Facebook. These people (almost 850 last time I checked) are avid fans of mine and caught up in reading the books. The group keeps the series in their minds even when the next book is months away. They ask me questions (why did you…, what inspired you…, what's going to happen to…, will you do a story about this or that character?), post songs and pictures that make them think of my characters, and become friends with each other and form a community online (and sometimes in person at events).

Twitter isn't something I do often (unless I'm working hard and avoiding addictive Facebook, but my Tweets feed to Facebook, where I usually engage more on them). I probably need to branch out more, but just don't have the time to learn anything new. I also participate in blog hops for themes that fit my series or interests, which brings new readers my way. Leagh also has arranged a couple of blog tours for me to promote my latest book at a number of book blogger sites. (In a blog tour, readers follow you from blog to blog over a set period of time as you share excerpts from a single scene or book or a series of blogs related to a single work; in a blog hop, there is a host blogger who lists all those participating and readers click from one blog to the next making the rounds. It brings a lot of new traffic to your site and it's good to do one a month if you can.)

Find ways to engage with readers face to face. In addition to the conference/convention circuit, if you're able to travel to these, just announce where you'll be and see who can show up. I did that on my way to a conference in New Orleans where I had a 3-hour layover at O'Hare in Chicago and three members of an online book club drove six hours round trip to hang out with me in the bar and talk about books (mine and others they loved).

In December 2012, I'm taking my daughter to New York City for a few days to celebrate her college graduation and am including an evening gathering with readers (about 20 from about five states have committed so far, although I haven't announced it in my newsletter yet, so it probably will grow). We'll hang out, eat, drink, and I'll sign print copies of my books for anyone wanting to buy the print versions, but will also sign e-reader covers or whatever they ask me to sign. These events are tax deductible, too, and I am looking for anything that will lower my income for tax purposes!

To sum up, write a series (preferably one with no end and one from the heart)! If you do a series, write an intro like *Masters at Arms* where you set up your series, your characters, and their initial conflicts. If you leave readers hanging with the intro and write well-edited, compelling reads thereafter, you will have fans for life who will put you on your auto-buy list.

Engage with readers in whatever social-media platform you enjoy and are comfortable with. Be real with them. And self publish! Quit giving publishers and agents the lion's share of your earnings!

About Kallypso Masters:

USA Today bestselling author Kallypso Masters writes emotional, realistic romance novels with dominant men and the women who bring them to their knees. (Mistress Grant being the exception, although she will bring her alpha man to his knees, as well.) The Doms/Domme at the Masters at Arms Club have been to hell and back, but Kally loves showing how there is never anyone so wounded he or she can't find true love. Readers often write to tell her how the books have changed their lives, or at the very least their perceptions of life and those around them.

Kally currently is working on bringing the first four books in the Rescue Me series to print (combining the first two books into one volume to keep the prices uniform and as low as possible for the four). The digital versions will be updated in December, as well.

Website: http://www.kallypsomasters.com/
Blog: http://kallypsomasters.blogspot.com/
Facebook: http://www.facebook.com/kallypsomasters,
https://www.facebook.com/KallypsoMastersAuthorPage,
and the series discussion group at
   https://www.facebook.com/groups/282370991862753/
Twitter: https://twitter.com/kallypsomasters

3
WE CAN
BY GIA BLUE

Yeah, my title says it all, but it's not what you think… I write hardcore smut. This isn't your momma's erotica and it sure as heck won't make it through the door of a traditional or electronic publisher. Nu-uh, never ever.

I write without boundaries, nothing is too taboo and if it gets my motors running, it goes on the page. I use insanely frank language that would make even the most seasoned publisher employed editors blush. And, hey, it may even squick them out solely based on my topics.

I bend the rules as far as I can and, in some cases, I've broken them. I am a smut-slinger and I won't apologize for it.

And that, right there, is why I self-publish. (Okay, I'm also pretty damned mercenary and I like the fact that I keep every penny earned, too.)

Now, don't get me wrong, traditional publishing (print or "e") has its place. I cut my teeth at electronic publishers, learned a shit-ton of amazing things from my editors, and enjoy the relationships I built with other authors during that time. I would not be the writer I am today without every single editor I've ever worked with. Period. Another thing to consider is your distribution possibilities. Publishers (typically) can get into eBook stores that are currently closed to self-publishing authors. It's cash they may not have earned on that book if they'd gone it alone.

At the same time… control over covers and release dates were out of my hands entirely. Sure, publishers may accept suggestions, but they tend to not let you do more than "suggest". Added to that is the fact that the time from sub (submission) to pub (publication) can be months. For some publishers, it's six months or more. That's six months that the manuscript is wasting away in the publishing queue when it could be earning you some well-deserved cash.

With self-publishing, I'm limited only by my writing speed, editor and cover artist. Since I write shorter works, I can (potentially) go from "The

End" to published in two weeks or less and, depending on the distributor, be paid for those sales within two months.

Notice that I listed editor and cover artist in the previous paragraph? Those two people are just as important in the self-publishing process as you are. I may write the story, but my editor will make it shine and the cover artist will help bring my story to reader-appealing life.

You need an editor. I don't care if you are the greatest author known to man, you need one. The average cost I found was a penny a word and yes, that can get expensive. But it's totally worth every dollar.

Now, for your cover, you could probably get away with buying a stock pic, using a free program like GIMP and then going on your merry way. I happen to be Photoshop savvy and do my own covers, but I've also found qualified, publisher employed artists whose prices start at fifty dollars.

So, if you write a ten thousand word short and snag a professional cover, you're looking at a minimum of one hundred fifty dollars. And I can't even guarantee that you'll earn enough to cover that cost.

Now, there's nothing stopping you from bypassing those expenses and going it on your own completely. Many have and many will.

And that's part of the reason there's a huge stigma surrounding self-published works. Not that *you'd* be like that, I'm just saying that an editor and cover artist will help you put your best foot forward as well as tug you from the pit-o-icky-self-published-stuffs.

I had my stuff edited, some better than others as I found my go-to peep, and have managed to be successful. Don't ask me how 'cause I have no idea. I started slinging smut on a lark as I saw hardcore erotica climb the Amazon charts.

Not long after I published my first few shorties, I hit it insanely big. My best seller hit number twenty-three on the Amazon Kindle Best Sellers list. Not for just erotica... no, that's overall. Out of 1.4 million eBooks, enough people bought Bent Over so that I could climb that high.

That right there is both staggering to me as well as insanely motivating.

Why? Because it proves that *we can*.

We can succeed.

We can flourish.

We can compete.

We can quit our day jobs and make a living.

I am living proof of those statements. I quit my job months ago (as of the writing of this article) and have happily more than replaced my daily grind income with my writing money.

In April 2012, I projected my income at just over ten thousand dollars. I won't have an accurate amount for several more weeks until Amazon's statement appears, but that's what I've estimated.

I'm not bragging. I'm not saying neener-neener.

I'm saying *we can*.

But wait!

Something else to consider is the fact that the ten thousand isn't *just* smut money. Nope, I write erotic romance (under a name you would have to wrestle from my cold, dead fingers) as well. Embrace diversity, nurture it, and watch it grow.

Self-publishing is publishing's future.

Will authors still submit to publishers? No doubt.

Like I said before, traditional and electronic publishers have their place in today's world, but I feel like their ability to respond to market shifts is lacking. The typical sub-to-pub is such a long process that even if you write about today's "it" topic today, the popularity will have crashed and burned before you book hits the shelf.

Are you going to be a best-seller today or a mid-lister six months from now?

I'm shooting for today.

Why?

Because I can.

About Gia Blue:

Gia Blue is a Top 100 Amazon Bestseller with over two dozen self-published books to her name, in addition to her work under another (secret) pen name. She makes a living as an author, and is blessed with an unbelievably dirty mind.

Website: www.GiaBlue.com
Twitter: http://twitter.com/smutastic
Facebook: http://facebook.com/smutastic

4
THE COVER: MAKE IT PROFESSIONAL!
BY H.P. MALLORY

Aside from the book itself, the most important component of your book is the cover. Why? Because it's the first touch point you and your potential reader share.

To understand what I mean, imagine this—you're looking for a paranormal romance book so you go to the Barnes and Noble website and do a search for "paranormal romance." Your eye is immediately drawn to the pictures on the page, not the text—this has been proven. People look at pictures and register them faster than they do text. That means your cover has to be interesting enough to: A) attract someone's attention; and B) attract their attention away from your competition.

The old adage that warns you not to "judge a book by its cover?" Yeah, well, that isn't true. Customers absolutely judge books by their covers—my readers tell me all the time that they first took a chance on my books because they were attracted by the covers. So what does this mean for you? It means you need a professional looking cover. Despite the fact that you're a self-published author, your cover should scream the opposite.

If it looks like Cousin Cindy Lou did it in Microsoft Paint, no one is going to buy it. If you don't believe me, try it. I dare you.

Okay, so hopefully I made my point that your cover needs to be professional. The best way to ensure the cover is professional is to (drum roll)... hire a professional. Don't make the mistake of letting a relative do it if they aren't graphic artists. If the cover doesn't come out well, it will hurt you significantly in the long run.

Let Your Name and Title Shine!

Okay, next tidbit...Because people are first drawn to images as opposed to text, it's important to ensure that your author name as well as the title of your book are legible. It's difficult to demonstrate this point with screen shots, since they are so much smaller than browsing books on Barnes and Noble, Amazon or Smashwords. Therefore, I advise you to go to these three websites and do some of your own searches and see which book titles and author names you can actually read.

The point I'm trying to make is: you want people to see your title and author name clearly, for a few reasons. First, remember that the reader's eyes are going to scan the image, so try to take advantage of that. Make your text clear and easy to read so everyone knows what book it is they're considering buying. Second, it establishes a form of relationship with the reader. If they see your book, read the title and/or your name and then see or hear about it again somewhere else, it helps to stoke that furnace in their memories. They'll automatically begin to remember your book image or title or your name and that will only help you later on. Also, for those who have read your first book and are unaware that your second book is available, by clearly advertising your name, you might ensure an instant sale!

Yes, there is an area to the right of the book image in the results pages on Barnes and Noble and Amazon which lists the title and your name independent of the cover. But why not maximize your chances by optimizing both locations?

Bragging Rights

Remember when you were growing up and everyone told you not to brag? Well, I'm here to say the opposite. Brag, brag, and then brag some more. What do I mean? Read on... Let's use my books as an example.

The feature I want you to notice is the area on the covers that says: "Bestselling Author."

That's my brag. Now, I didn't just make that up and slap it on there, hoping it might come true. I actually made it to the Kindle and Nook bestseller lists; so technically, I am a "bestselling author." I wanted to add that little credential to my books to shout it to the world because it's another way to tell potential readers that they should take a chance on my books. And in a universe of 800,000 + e-books which continues to expand daily, trust me, you'll need all the help you can get!

Let's say you haven't made it to the bestseller list, but you're a bestseller in a category. Absolutely add that! I could have included something like: bestselling author of Fantasy—or something similar.

Any kudos you can mention, you absolutely should. Of course, there is an exception, as in all rules... If the only accolade you ever received is a gold star on your eighth grade book report, you probably shouldn't include it...

What Book Number Is This, For God's Sake!!!

The thing to remember when creating your covers or the description page of your books is to make everything easy on the reader. That means if you are writing books in a series, please do everyone the enormous favor of telling us where your particular book falls in the sequence.

With my book covers, I've spelled out where each book falls in my series by stating "Book 2 of the Dulcie O'Neil Series" or "Book 2 of the Jolie Wilkins Series." Unless you're the Easter Bunny passing out chocolate eggs, don't make your reader go on a hunt or they're likely to get annoyed which could mean a lost sale for you.

Advertise your other books

Do you have another bestselling book or a book you'd like to draw attention to? If so, you can mention that book on your cover. I'm sure you've seen this on plenty of traditionally published books. Actually, on my book coming out with Random House in February 2012, titled Witchful Thinking, it clearly states on the cover:

"Author of Fire Burn and Cauldron Bubble"

Now, you'll probably notice that I didn't do this on any of my self-published books but that's not to say it isn't a good idea. I actually ran out of space, otherwise I would have.

Use the popularity of another author

Ever see those quotes from well known authors on books you're considering reading? Well, those quotes are there for a really good reason—if you recognize the name of the person offering the recommendation, you're more inclined to want to purchase and read the book.

Therefore, if you know a Stephen King equivalent and that person is willing to read your book and comment positively about it, absolutely use that to your advantage and include the quote on your book cover.

Um, any Stephen King or equivalents out there who would like to comment on my books? Please feel free!

The Cover In Review
- Hire a professional to create your cover
- Allow your book cover to stand out from others in your genre
- Make sure your title and author name are clearly legible on your book cover
- Include any bragging rights
- If your book is in a series, make sure you include the book number
- Advertise your other books
- Include quotes pertinent to your book from well known authors

This article is excerpted from H.P. Mallory's book <u>Quit Your Day Job, A Guide for the Self Published Author</u> (http://amzn.to/JcmA3o).

About H.P. Mallory:

New York Times and *USA Today* Bestselling Urban Fantasy & Paranormal Romance Author H.P. Mallory started her writing career as a self-published author and hit both the Amazon and the Barnes and Noble bestseller's lists with her two series, the Jolie Wilkins series and the Dulcie O'Neil series.

She signed with Random House (Bantam imprint) to write three books in the Jolie Wilkins series (Witchful Thinking, The Witch is Back and Something Witchy This Way Comes). Now she loves the fact that she's both a traditionally published author as well as a self-published one (with her Dulcie O'Neil series).

Her interests are varied but aside from writing, she's most excited about traveling. She feels extremely fortunate to have been able to live in England and Scotland, both places really having a profound effect on her books.

H.P. Mallory wants you to stay in touch!

Website: http://hpmallory.com/
On Facebook: http://www.facebook.com/hpmallory
On Twitter: http://twitter.com/hpmallory
Mailing list sign up: http://hpmallory.com/contact/

5
THE BUSINESS OF PUBLISHING:
AN INTERVIEW OF SHOSHANNA EVERS
BY AUTHOR CARA BRISTOL

This interview was original posted in two parts on erotic romance author Cara Bristol's website at www.CaraBristol.com in 2012.

Cara Bristol: Ellora's Cave published Shoshanna Evers' first book Punishing the Art Thief in September 2010. Since then this RN and married mom of a young son has released FOURTEEN titles and quit her day job. She's in several anthologies (one a print release of three of her EC titles) and recently expanded into the realm of self-publishing, producing six titles, among them the Amazon Erotica Bestselling short story Overheated, a new Femme Dom series, and the #1 Amazon Authorship Bestselling nonfiction book How to Write Hot Sex. In addition to Ellora's Cave, she's published with The Wild Rose Press, Cleis Press (Best Bondage Erotica 2012) and Berkley Heat (Agony/Ecstasy). I wanted to pick Shoshanna's brain about the business side of writing because clearly she's doing something right.

Cara Bristol: When you sold your first romance, Punishing the Art Thief, did you know then that you wanted to switch careers from nursing to writing? At what point did that become the goal?

Shoshanna Evers: I wrote my first novel when I was nineteen, long before I ever started nursing school. That first novel is terrible and will never see the light of day... The second book I wrote was an early version of Hollywood Spank, which as you know is not the first book that got published. Nursing was more of the back-up plan if things didn't work out with writing.

Cara Bristol: How much has the potential salability of a book affected your choice of what to write? Do you simply write whatever you want or do you consider how well you think it might sell?

Shoshanna Evers: I definitely have my readers in mind before I start writing. I'll make changes to a book if I think my readership won't like a certain aspect, for example. But ultimately I write what gets me hot and what stirs my emotions, in the hopes that my readers will feel the same way.

Cara Bristol: What has been your most successful title/book? Why do you think that is?

Shoshanna Evers: My most successful book is Overheated, a 5K word short erotic romance story - it's been on the Amazon Erotica Bestseller list for a while now. At first it got on the list and then it would fall off every other day, but lately it's held strong. I haven't been counting the weeks/months because I don't want to jinx it, but it's bound to end at some point. I never expected Overheated to strike such a chord with people. I wish I knew exactly what it was about that story that makes it so popular so I could replicate its success, but unfortunately there's a substantial amount of luck involved, I think. Also – success breeds success. If the book gets on a bestseller list, more people will notice it so more people buy it, which pushes it up the list, which makes more people notice it, so more people buy it, etcetera. In other words, a popular book gets onto a bestseller list, but being on a bestseller list will increase its popularity.

Cara Bristol: How has having an agent made your life easier? At what point do you think an author should seek representation?

Shoshanna Evers: I enjoy having a business-minded woman with a stake in my success (my agent) to bounce ideas off of. And she's taken a look at contracts for me even when she's not taking her cut, which is nice. When I was working on a book for a publisher that ended up falling through for various reasons, it was great to have her send emails on my behalf so I could remain "the author" instead of "the woman who wants to sell something". Lately I've been focusing a lot on my self-published books because that's where I've been finding the most success, personally, and with it the most money. (**Editorial Update**: my agent got me a six-book deal with Simon & Schuster, so I'm actively balancing both trad-pub and self-pub now)

I'm not sure when an author should seek representation. I guess when she's written a book that she wants to have traditionally published. Otherwise, what's the point?

Cara Bristol: Other than improving craft, if a writer did nothing else, what three things should she do to further her career?

Shoshanna Evers: Three things other than improve your craft?

One: Promote your books, and if you have no books, promote yourself. Make it so everyone knows your name because that leads to sales.

Two: Stay current on what's happening in the publishing industry. Read blogs and articles and books about it. You'd be surprised how confused new writers can get about the business side of writing, but ultimately writing is just one part of the job. More than half of my work day is spent on business, not writing.

Three: Get to know your readers. I'm constantly on Twitter and Facebook so I can interact with my readers and other writers (who, by the way, are also readers! You just have to look at my Kindle book list to see that's true for me too, LOL). Readers expect a certain level of responsiveness from an author, and I completely understand that. Recently I read a book I loved, so I went online, Googled the author's name to find her website, and looked for the "contact" button so I could tell her what a great book she wrote. There was no email listed. No Twitter account. No Facebook. I was quite surprised… and she missed out on some fan mail, LOL. I was all ready to squee, too…

Cara Bristol: You were already multi-published when you began putting out some indie books. Why did you decide to self-publish some works? What is the determining factor whether you seek a publisher or produce it yourself?

Shoshanna Evers: I decided to self-publish some works because I heard Amazon was giving 70% royalties based on list price. It's as simple as that. I love my publishers dearly, but writing is also a business so I made a business decision to see how self-publishing might work for me. I think if I didn't have the platform Ellora's Cave helped me build I wouldn't have anywhere near the success I've had with self-publishing. I'll always be grateful to them for giving me my start, and even after I started self-publishing I did publish Bedhead with them, which came out in November 2011.

As for when an author should seek a publisher or self-publish, I think it might be beneficial to have at least your first book published by a traditional or small press publisher. That way it proves to yourself and to your readers that you have what it takes, so to speak, and that you're not self-publishing just because no one else would take your work. I'm so glad that Amazon KDP didn't exist when I was first starting out, because I never would have grown as a writer. The only thing that made me grow as a writer was getting those rejection letters and realizing I had a lot to learn. I took writing classes, I subjected my drafts to brutal critique groups, and I kept submitting my manuscripts. I just kept writing. If I had been able to easily self-pub back in those days, I'd have a lot of unpolished books out there.

Cara Bristol: What factors should a writer look for in selecting a publisher?

Shoshanna Evers: There are two main factors I can think of: Do you personally read a lot of that particular publishing imprint's books? If the answer is yes, then you know that you like their books and they probably accept the type of book you wrote, and you know there's an audience of readers out there (like you) who are buying their books. The other factor is: what does their contract look like? Do you have to option your first born son? Do you have to promise never to publish another book in that category again because it might compete with the contracted book? etc. Look at the option and non-compete clauses and also look at when and how you can get your rights back if things don't work out the way you hoped. I'm not a lawyer and this isn't contract advice, it's just common sense. #disclaimer

Cara Bristol: What mistakes do you see authors making in their writing careers?

Shoshanna Evers: I see writers who aren't ready to have books out there self-publishing. I recently read a self-published book that was an amazing story, but my reading experience was ruined by the author's less-than-stellar writing skills. If she'd waited until she'd grown as a writer before publishing the book, it could have been a bestseller. Another mistake I see authors making is they brand themselves based on one book (usually their first book or the name of their series) instead of on their author name. For example, having a Twitter handle that focuses on the title of their book, and then they come out with another book and they have to completely rebrand.

Cara Bristol: What mistakes have you've made?

Shoshanna Evers: I'm probably too open and honest online. I don't keep any sense of mystery. You guys always know when I'm on a diet or when I'm ready for a nap or when my writing is slow-going, LOL. Everyone makes mistakes, it's part of the learning curve. Every time I sent out a manuscript that wasn't good because I didn't have the skill yet to *know* that it wasn't good enough could be considered a mistake, too. In a few years I'm going to look at something I'm doing now and shake my head at how stupid I am, because I'll have learned something new that I don't yet know.

Cara Bristol: What do you think you've done right?

Shoshanna Evers: I think I'm pretty good at the marketing aspect of writing. My sales are relatively strong - I usually sell well over a thousand books a month and sometimes over two thousand. It's not because I'm such an incredible writer (although I have put in my dues), rather I think it's just because I'm not afraid to remind people that I have books available for sale. I buy books several times a week based on other people's taglines and links I see on Twitter, so I know it works, LOL. I'm hoping with the four new books I just released (The Dominatrix Fantasy Trilogy and the trilogy set) that my sales numbers will increase. (**Editorial update**: They have! Oh my gosh, they have. Thank you to my readers, *muah*)

The other thing I think I've done right is I write books without censoring myself. If I think something is really hot, I'll write it, even if it's the sort of the thing I'd be completely embarrassed for anyone else to know that I think is sexy. It makes for awkward conversations with people who know me in real life, because they have a window into my dirty mind.

Cara Bristol: What promotional activities have been successful for you?

Shoshanna Evers: I have a Twitter handle (@ShoshannaEvers), a Facebook page (http://www.facebook.com/shoshanna.evers), an author website www.ShoshannaEvers.com, a blog www.TheWritersChallenge.com and a book website for my non-fiction book www.HowToWriteHotSex.com.

I blog and I guest blog and I do interviews like this one. I solicit reviews for my books (but not nearly as often as I should. If you're a book reviewer, email me!). I have a newsletter that goes out when I have a new release (sign up on my website where it says Subscribe to Newsletter). And I try to thank my readers on a daily basis online. (Which reminds me…thank you. You guys are the reason I write.)

Cara Bristol: Which promotional activities have *not* been successful?

Shoshanna Evers: Hard to say, but I don't think I get as many sales from guest blogging as I do from promo Tweets. I still do it though to keep my name out there. Also, I once tried putting the first chapter of Snowed In With the Tycoon at the end of Overheated, and that didn't work so I took it off.

Cara Bristol: Where would you like your career to be in five years?

Shoshanna Evers: I'm branching out into some other aspects of publishing. I've signed an NDA (non-disclosure agreement) so that's all I can say on that for the time being. But I've got big plans ;) (**Editorial Update:** If you're reading this book, you know that my Big Secret was to create the website www.SelfPubBookCovers.com to bring indie authors and cover artists together so indie authors could get quality book covers, instantly, at a low price.)

As for my books, I have a compulsion to write so I don't see that slowing down anytime soon. Maybe in five years one of my books will hit the New York Times Bestseller list. (**2014 Update:** Goal achieved, thanks to my awesome readers!) That would be cool, just to have that in my bio, LOL. But somehow I don't see The Dominatrix Fantasy Trilogy ending up on the *NYT* list. It's just too taboo. Then again, whoever could have imagined the success of 50 Shades of Grey? (Not to go off on a tangent, but I'm thrilled that the 50 Shades trilogy brought so much mainstream attention to the erotic romance genre!)

Cara Bristol: What career advice would you give an intermediate-level author (i.e. one who has already published a few titles)?

Shoshanna Evers: My advice would be to keep writing, because building your backlist is a good way to build your income. The more titles you have for sale the more chances you have of connecting with a reader. I would also suggest that an author who has several traditionally and small-press published books might want to try self-publishing. I think that self-publishing is the wave of the future. But don't do it unless you're ready to treat it like you're running a business. Don't use your kid brother's cover art just because you'll hurt his feelings if you don't. You need to be able to look at your work objectively, and ask other people for their opinion if you can't get enough distance from your own work. I see so many self-published books out there with crappy covers, and it's a shame because that's an aspect that you have a lot of control over when you choose to self-publish.

My other advice would be to remind your readers that you have books for sale and give us some links! I chat with authors on Twitter who only promote on release day, and even then they do it with a real sense of embarrassment, like telling their readers about a book they might want to read is dirty business. But I love a well-crafted tag line and I click links all the time. If the free sample download is good I buy the book, period. Sometimes I follow authors on Twitter and I have *no idea* that they're authors unless I happen to look at their bios, because they never mention their books! Don't be one of those.

My last bit of advice might be controversial. Personally, I usually try to avoid getting into politics online because I don't want to lose a reader over some self-righteous blog post. It's hard for people (myself included) to separate the book from the author. If the author pisses them off, they won't want to buy her book no matter how good it sounds. Occasionally I let something slip, but in general I don't use my author platform as a platform for soapboxing about politics. I'm not sure if soapboxing is a word. Fortunately, I get to make up words for a living, so I'm keeping it. ;)

Thanks for interviewing me, Cara! :)

Please stay in touch. I welcome emails from readers and writers.

Email: shoshannaevers@gmail.com

Website: www.ShoshannaEvers.com (sign up for my New Releases Newsletter on the right side of the page at ShoshannaEvers.com/blog for a newsletter filled with sneak peeks, excerpts, amazing deals, and my new releases!)

Blog: www.TheWritersChallenge.com

Twitter: https://twitter.com/ShoshannaEvers

Facebook: http://www.facebook.com/shoshanna.evers

6
I DID IT MY WAY
BY LIZ MATIS

After receiving a request for a full manuscript from one of the Big 6 Publishers, Playing For Keeps lingered in submission limbo for over two years. Yes, two years. About eighteen months in the Junior Editor who requested the manuscript emailed me that she loved my voice and was sending Playing For Keeps to the Senior Editor. Seven months later the manuscript was rejected, the Senior Editor didn't feel the same way.

During this time I did what any good writer does – completed another manuscript.

Did I want to wait another two years to hear yay or nay on Love By Design?

Nay.

If I were going the self-published route I was all in. Why not try a small press? I was frustrated with the submission process. Each press had different requirements and then there was the waiting game all over again. And frankly from the blogs I frequent those small presses weren't making much money for their authors, which means they're not reaching readers. With Amazon's KDP program, Barnes and Noble's Pubit program and Smashwords, I knew I could do better. And I have.

Before I did anything I read up on self-publishing. Blogs like J.A. Konrath and WG2E provided a wealth of information.

Informed I jumped in. While I waited for my manuscript to come back from the proofreader I set up a dba by getting a business certificate with my local government, set up my business checking account, and purchased 10 ISBN numbers through R.R. Bowker.

Upon the return of my manuscript from the proofreader, I read it over again and caught a couple of things she missed. I advise you to do the same.

Can you learn to format? Yes, but for me the learning curve would be steep. I asked myself wouldn't your limited time be better spent writing?

The answer for me was yes.

Can you learn to design a cover? Yes, but my attempts – I'll admit – were lackluster. I found a book cover designer who specialized in romance. Not only did she give me three great covers, she did what I never thought of doing – branding the books with a style that screamed my tag line - Fun, Flirty, and Fiery Romps.

I run the production side like a business so I think it's important to set a budget and then within that budget decide how to proceed. Like any new business venture you must invest money for start-up costs. When I moved money from my regular savings to my business checking account I said to myself, "I'm making an investment in me." That investment paid off.

Now I leave twenty-five percent of my royalties in my business checking for future productions of my books and other business related expenses like conferences. The other seventy-five percent goes into my business savings.

Book sales at first were slow, but picked up after two months. Playing For Keeps hit as high as #2 on the Kindle Best Seller List in Sports Fiction. In the UK it went as high as #14. Love By Design has steady sales and great reviews. My third release, Going For It, hit the #1 spot in Sports Fiction and then broke into the Top 100 Contemporary Romance List. For social media I have a blog, a Twitter and Facebook account. I highly recommend setting up a Goodreads author account.

Because of the success of Playing For Keeps, a narrator approached me about producing an audiobook. The ACX.com website (Audiobook Creation Exchange) is part of the Amazon family so you use your Amazon account sign on and the website finds your books and you 'grab' them. The instructions are easy to follow. You can wait for narrators to audition for you or you can listen to narrators and approach them with an offer. The narrator basically does everything—narrates, produces, and uploads the audiobook. Royalties are shared 50/50 with no upfront cost to the author. I can't lose! The Playing For Keeps audiobook was released on 9/13/12 and hit the Audible Chick Lit Best Seller List.

Authors ask me if I'll ever submit again to a publisher. My answer, for now, is no. I like doing it my way.

About Liz Matis:

Liz Matis is a bestseller in Sports Fiction for both Playing For Keeps and Going For it and a bestseller in Media Tie-In for Love By Design on Amazon. She's focused solely on self-publishing.

Reviewers have said of Playing For Keeps, "you will get a wildly sexy romance with depth and laughs…an engaging storyline that will keep readers turning the pages." In Love By Design "readers will get a kick out of these characters…fans of any Real Housewives will enjoy the ride."

Liz read her first romance at the age of fifteen and soon after that wrote her first romances for friends starring them and their latest crushes.

Liz Matis wants you to stay in touch!

Smashwords: https://www.smashwords.com/books/view/95177
Blog: http://www.taoofliz.blogspot.com
Twitter: @LizMatis
Facebook: http://on.fb.me/TVGoX0
Goodreads: http://www.goodreads.com/author/show/5289185.Liz_Matis
Email: elizabetmatis@gmail.com

7
RESPECT YOUR READERS
BY KATRIENA KNIGHTS

I've been published in ebook format since ebooks were practically in diapers, landing my first contract with the now-defunct Dreams Unlimited in 1999. I didn't jump into self-publishing quite so early in the game, but I did start a bit ahead of the current rush. I put my backlist book, *My Cyber Valentine,* which had reached the end of its contract at Loose Id, up in paperback and pdf on Lulu when the concept was still being eyed askance by most "serious" authors. Since that first experiment, I've put several backlist books and short stories as well as new short stories and collections up on numerous self-publishing venues, including Amazon, Barnes & Noble, All Romance eBooks and 1 Place for Romance. Have I made a bazillion dollars? No. Have I created new opportunities for work that otherwise might never have seen the light of day? Absolutely. I've also been able to help a few other people get their books and stories out to new venues—some of whom have had even better results than I have.

After some experimenting and tweaking, self-publishing has become a regular part of my repertoire. I continue to pursue traditional publishing, and the majority of my books still come out through small, independent publishers like Changeling Press and Samhain. My romance books tend to sell better through these more traditional outlets. However, short stories and collections in other genres tend to sell better when I self-publish. So I tend to send romance books to the publishers I work with on a regular basis and put fantasy, science fiction and urban fantasy shorts and collections out into the world on my own. Electronic editions sell better than paperbacks, in my experience, though I have some plans to experiment a bit more with the paperback format in the near future.

To prepare my stories for publication, I make my own cover art and do my own conversions. I don't trust my own eyes for editing, so I have other folks look manuscripts over for me. I don't hire out for extensive editing for short stories, although I'll probably have to look into that if I end up self-publishing original, novel-length works. So far all my full-length, self-published books have been backlist and so have already been edited, so I usually just give them a quick once-over before finalizing the manuscripts.

I fully expect self-publishing to remain an important part of my career. It's certainly not going away any time soon, and as writers and agents get more comfortable with the new paradigms—well, as soon as the new paradigms settle in to stay a while—the independent author will become as much a driving force in the industry as the independent musician is in the music industry. Independent publishing provides a place for writers whose work doesn't fit into the pigeonholes major publishers have developed to categorize books for their marketing teams. Readers who want something that can't be easily categorized will be able to find it; writers who want to produce something that's aimed at a smaller audience than a traditional publisher can support will be able to find that audience and give them a high quality product.

The key here is "high quality product." The best advice I can offer those embarking on self-publishing is to respect your readers. Don't give them anything but your best. Don't rush your work or skip steps just because you can. Beyond respecting your readers, respect your work. Whether it's a romance or a thriller or a poetry chapbook or a short story, that piece deserves everything you can do to bring it to its highest potential. If that means hiring an editor to help you find your blind spots, then do that. If it means putting a manuscript in a drawer for a few months so you can ruminate on it, do that. If you don't feel confident enough about a story to send it to a traditional publisher, then you shouldn't feel confident enough to send it out to the world at large, either.

That's not to say that you shouldn't pursue self-publishing if you're already traditionally published, or that you should avoid traditional publishing if you're successful with your independent efforts. The writing career of the future is likely to consist of a combination of both approaches, plus a variety of other income streams such as public speaking, workshops, blogging income and other types of freelance ventures. The verbal battles between the traditional and indy camps are pointless and counterproductive. One approach is not better than the other across the board. Your job as a writer in these bizarre, mutating times is to figure out what combination works best for you, and then pursue that. Your combination might not be best for another writer, and we all should respect that.

So, if you haven't tried self-publishing before, my advice is to give it a whirl and see how it goes for you. If you're already in the independent trenches, keep plugging. The future is here, and I think it's all kind of cool.

About Katriena Knights:

Katriena Knights is the author of several contemporary and paranormal romances. As Elizabeth Jewell, she writes m/m erotic romance, and as KC Myers she has published science fiction, fantasy and urban fantasy. She lives in Colorado with her two children, a goofy dog, two ferrets and a weird little gerbil.

Keep in touch!
http://www.katrienaknights.com
Blog: http://katrienaknights.blogspot.com
Twitter: http://twitter.com/crazywritinfool
Facebook: http://www.facebook.com/KatrienaKnightsAuthor

8
10, NO *11* SUCCESSFUL SELF-PUBLISHING TIPS I WISH I'D KNOWN
BY HEATHER THURMEIER

1. Successful self-publishing is time consuming. It's not just writing a story one day then sticking it up on Amazon, Smashwords and Barnes & Noble the next while you drink a beer and celebrate a job well done. Regardless of how fast you write it, it's also time spent editing, formatting, blurbing, cover art designing, marketing, and bookkeeping. Whew. Are you tired yet?

2. Successful self-publishing a book takes many, *many* rewrites to get everything *just* right. And some of those rewrites might be huge, gigantic beasts, and they make take days or weeks or months to complete, but they will also make your book the best it can be. And isn't the best book you can write the one you want to publish?

3. Successful self-publishing doesn't come with a form rejection letter. You may have heard every author who's ever submitted their work to a publishing house or agent gets one of those. But self-published authors don't. Nope… You have to HUNT ONE DOWN and wrangle it into your book's process. You have to give your book—your *baby*—to a trusted friend or family member, or better yet a writing colleague and ask them to critique it for you. And then you cross your fingers and hope they tell you honestly where your book blows chunks because if they don't, the reviewers will.

4. Successful self-publishing your own book takes courage. It's hard to put yourself out there for the world to see. It's a giant game of "Will they like me?" and "Will I be good enough?" "Will I be picked last for kick-ball again?" all over again and you have to be strong enough to survive it. You have to be brave enough to take the chance to go through with it and hit that publish button.

5. Successful self-publishing means you have to be your own advocate.

No one else is going to look out for you or your career. You have to make sure your book is the best it can be before it goes live for the world—yes, the WORLD!!—to buy it. That means you may have to take a step back from jumping in with both feet. You may have to take a couple of classes or webinars or even attend a writing conference. You have to be the one to recognize what's lacking in your masterpiece. To do that, you need to perfect your craft. You have to find your shortcomings and fix them because you don't have the safety net of a publishing house to catch your mistakes. No one's going to tell you that you've left your participles dangling (If you find any in this article, blame my editor. LOL) or that your use of the word "juxtaposition" is out of context. You have to do that and if you can't, there's a class for that. Find it, take it, apply what you've learned.

6. Successful self-publishing means you have to be your own banker. You have to put up the money to make your book happen or you have to do everything yourself. Are you ready to commit the time or money to this venture? Are you ready to invest in your future by putting in a solid effort now? Because half-assing it isn't going to cut it in the self-publishing game.

7. Successful self-publishing means after you tell people you self-published that book you've been working on for the last X number of years, you're going to see The Look on their faces. It's not a good look. It's the look that tells you they doubt the quality of your writing. You couldn't hack it in the big leagues so you had to publish it yourself, right? You couldn't score an agent with that lackluster, dried-up plot so you decided to stick it up on Amazon to make a quick buck, didn't you? Prove them wrong. Don't do it that way or for those reasons. Self-publish your book because it's good. And not just "my mom says it's the best book she ever, ever read" good. Refer back to tip five and make sure you do that. Then when your baby is really ready, publish it and tell your doubter friends to read it before they judge it and no they can't have a free copy. ;) Hey, I need that 70% royalty to fund my next book release!

8. Successful self-publishing means you may put your book—your beautiful 300-page baby of your heart, love-fest—up for sale and…you might not make any money. Yep. It's true. I know it's hard to believe. I know it sucks to see those single digit sales roll in every few days…or so. But that's a distinct possibility. You may not be Mr/Mrs Next Big Thing in the self-publishing world and you need to be okay with that going in.

9. Successful self-publishing might force you to make tough choices. But you have to. YOU have to ensure that your book is the best it can be. So what if it's not selling? What then? Where's the marketing wiz to help you stimulate your sales? Look in the mirror, you found them. That might mean you have to make tough choices you don't want to make. It might mean you have to stop paying for advertising on your BFF's blog because people aren't clicking through the cover link. It might mean your loved one who slaved over your cover art for hours on the computer one night while watching a slasher movie might have to make it again. Or you might have to hire a professional cover artist.

10. Successful self-publishing is all about creating a network. I recently heard someone say "it takes a village to sell a book." Build your village now and keep building it. Use social media like twitter, Facebook, Goodreads, and Pinterest (among countless others) to build your relationships with readers and other writers. This DOES NOT mean shoving your book down your followers throats. Along with social media, network with writing organizations and other writers at conferences. Build those lasting relationships with others in your genre and you've not only found new friends with a similar passion in life, but you've also found someone to cross-promote with. Ah-ha!

11. A bonus tip! Self-publishing means YOU are the one who determines your level of success. Maybe your success is measured by your sales rank. Maybe it's by your number of 5-star reviews. Maybe it's making an Amazon best-seller list in your category. Or maybe it's simply the fact that you took the story of your heart, molded it, shaped it, nurtured it and finally believed in your own abilities enough to publish it that makes you successful as a self-published author. But whatever your measure of success, choose it for you. Judge yourself on your own merits and not on the success or failure of others.

About Heather Thurmeier:

Amazon Bestselling, multi-published, agented author Heather Thurmeier writes humorous contemporary romances. She's been published with Silver Publishing, Crimson Romance, and also enjoys self-publishing her own titles.

Carly Phillips, *NY Times* Bestselling Author says, "Heather Thurmeier's hunky heroes and feisty heroines will have you laughing out loud, falling in love ... and coming back for more!"

New York Times and *USA Today* bestselling author Jennifer Probst says, "Heather Thurmeier writes sweet, funny romances that capture your heart!"

Heather Thurmeier is a lover of strawberry margaritas, a hater of spiders, and a reality TV junkie. She was born and raised in the Canadian prairies, but now lives in upstate New York with her own personal romance Hero (aka her husband) and their two little princesses. When she's not busy taking care of the kids and an adventurous puppy named Indy, Heather's hard at work on her next romance novel.

Heather Thurmeier wants you to stay in touch!

Website: http://heatherthurmeier.com
Blog: http://heatherthurmeier.com
Twitter: https://twitter.com/hthurmeier
Facebook: http://www.facebook.com/HeatherThurmeierAuthor
Goodreads: http://www.goodreads.com/author/show/5211580.Heather_Thurmeier
Email: heatherthurmeier@gmail.com

9
A DOG, A NEW GENRE, AND A CHARITY
BY JENNIFER PROBST

When self-publishing exploded onto the market, I watched certain books sail up the bestseller ranks, and read numerous articles touting the tons of money finally pouring into poverty stricken writer's pockets. I measured the good with the bad, but was never personally attached to the concept of self-publishing my books. My goal was to obtain a solid reputable publisher and grow my career in the romance industry. My passion was writing romance and I rarely strayed off genre.

Until the dog's voice.

Happily writing my new work in progress, I became haunted by a dog's voice. The dog talked to me at night, throughout the day, and yipped at me when I awoke. Now, first off to clarify, I am a huge dog lover. I own two rescue dogs, volunteer at the local shelter, and adore reading books where dogs are the main protagonist. But writing about dogs was not my goal in life, and I never thought of writing something that wasn't a romance.

Back to the dog.

I lived with the voice for two weeks. Finally, I complained to my friend that I didn't know what to do. She suggested I write his story in order to gain some peace and quiet. This made sense, so I finally sat at my desk and listened to his narrative.

His story amazed and humbled me. As I viewed the pages, I realized I needed to share this story with readers, and began a quest to see where I can could publish it.

I came up with nothing.

Dog magazines weren't the right market. The story was super short, and most places required certain word count. Most of my queries weren't answered, and I became faced with a common dilemma among writers. Stick the story in a drawer and move on? Publish it on my blog? Or keep searching?

I finally reached the perfect solution. I would self-publish the story myself. I decided to charge .99, publish it via Kindle, and send half of the proceeds to the animal shelter I worked with. I was always struggling for a way to give the center more, but had limited funds. This was a perfect way to share my story with the world and give back to the shelter.

I scoured the photo sites for a perfect cover, studied up on formatting, and did my homework. I sent the story out for some beta reads, and then had it edited for content by a few trusted authors. Because it was a short story, it only took a few days for me to find the learning curve before I pushed the button.

My story had been published.

I did some local social media for publicity, wrote a blog post, and had some friends spread the word. Then I booked some local talks through the library to talk about writing in a dog's voice and my experience with shelters and self-publishing.

Slowly, the book began moving up Amazon in its category and after a few months, it hung at the number one spot. Right next to my own personal hero: The Dog Whisperer.

Because of the story's success, I then published it with Smashwords so it would be available on other eformats. The reviews that trickled in were positive, and the story began to grow almost organically from word of mouth.

Since I published the story one year ago, I am thrilled to report I am now able to write out a very nice check to the shelter every month. I am currently averaging net sales of $1000 per month. I receive mail from readers who say his story touched them and made a difference. Without the option of self-publishing, I don't think his story would have been shared, and the pages would wither in my desk drawer.

For me, self-publishing was a very personal way of changing genre, pushing my limits, and giving back to my well loved charity.

About Jennifer Probst:

Jennifer Probst is a *New York Times* and *USA Today* bestselling romance author. She's been published with Gallery Books/Simon & Schuster, Entangled, Decadent, Red Sage, and The Wild Rose Press. She has also co-written a children's book with her twelve year old niece titled *Buffy and the Carrot*. Her self-published short story about a shelter dog, *A Life Worth Living*, donates part of the proceeds from sales to a local animal shelter.

Reviewers have said, "Make way for the superbly talented Jennifer Probst!" (Maldivian Book Reviewers).

Jennifer makes her home in Upstate New York with the whole crew. Her two young sons keep her active, stressed, joyous, and sad her house will never be truly clean.

Jennifer Probst wants you to stay in touch!

Smashwords: http://www.smashwords.com/books/view/91302
Website: http://www.jenniferprobst.com
Twitter: https://twitter.com/#!/jenniferprobst
Facebook: http://www.facebook.com/#!/jenniferprobst.authorpage
Goodreads: http://www.goodreads.com/author/show/2965489
Email: romancewriter121@yahoo.com

10
A TALE OF TWO NOVELLAS
BY SKYE WARREN

With the accessibility of self-publishing, authors have more freedom and possibility than ever. But that resultant proliferation, combined with a tightening economy overall, mean we also face more competition and rejections.

Every author reaches the crossroads sooner or later, to self-publish or seek traditional publication, but both of them lead to the same place. We are writing the books of our hearts, but also writing to the expectations of our audiences.

I wrote a novella to sell. It fit neatly within a popular genre: contemporary erotic romance. The characters were flawed enough to be interesting, but ultimately fit into the romance cannon: beautiful, strong and kind-hearted. I wrote in third person POV, mimicking the writing style that is common. Through two critique groups, over a dozen fellow writers helped me tighten up the prose, deepen the characterization, tidy up the plot.

I wrote another novella on the side, never expecting it to be read. This was a dark erotic thriller, although it doesn't quite fit into that genre, nor is that a particularly popular genre even if it did. It is violent and depressing, indulging the very darkest parts of me. I wrote it for myself, in first person POV and in a sort of contemplative, almost stream-of-consciousness style. It was critiqued by no one.

As a budding writer, I read all about marketing and promotion. It seemed that people on both sides, self-published or traditionally published, lamented about how hard it was to get noticed by readers. Popular wisdom says that poor ratings are the author's fault, a result of bad writing. But poor *sales*, those are a result of lack of marketing efforts by publishers or wonky rating systems from booksellers. Those darn readers just won't find our books!

I wondered how hard it really was for an unknown author to break through the invisibility barrier? How many sales would a book make if no one knew about it? At heart, I am a scientist, and so I put it to the test.

I threw both novellas up for sale.

The covers were mostly just stock images with titles slapped on top. Breaking the respectable self-publishing author's credo, I paid no editor to proofread them. Formatting was nonexistent. I took what I had and ran it through the online meatgrinders.

How bad was it? I was too afraid to download it onto my own reading device, for fear of what I would see. That bad.

But it was just a little experiment. Even though I had a small group of friends on twitter and a few subscribers on my budding author's blog, I created a separate identity for this. I told *no one* about it. After all, doing so would have compromised the experiment.

And I waited.

At the end of the month, when the novellas had been up for two weeks, I had sold around 100 copies. It wasn't going to break any records, but it told me that discovery did happen. Those sales amounted to $69. I write erotica, so I figured it was a sign.

What shocked me, though, was how far the dark piece outsold the more conventional one. The market for the more conventional one was so much bigger, many times over. And yet, my dark little novella, riddled with editing errors and confusing plot twists and horrifying subject matter, made the bulk of the money.

It had to be a fluke. I remade the cover for the low performer. I fixed up the blurb. I sent it out to some review sites. The following month, I sold over 300 copies total, most of them of the darker novella.

Damn.

Determined, I threw up a quick website and blog. At the prompting of a reader's email, I created a twitter account. I participated in a few memes and blog hops to drive traffic my way.

I picked out a short story I had written, a little 5,000-word story piece, cleaned it up, and put it up for free. It took off, reaching the #1 free spot on All Romance Ebooks right away and the #1 free spot on Amazon's Erotica free bestseller list shortly after. This story was an erotic romance, I reasoned, right in line with my lonely little novella. The people who downloaded and raved about my story would be interested in the light novella.

Sure enough, at the end of the month, I had sold over 800 copies. Not of the light book though. Overwhelmingly, the dark piece was the winner.

Now I felt guilty. Here I was, supposedly an author who cared about craft, peddling a story with no editing. And no, I am not one of those writers who writes clean from Draft One. This story was a mess, and people were paying me for it! They mentioned poor editing in their reviews and marked down for it, but the sales kept coming.

Even though I'd started this whole thing on a whim, I didn't want to stop. So I hired a copyeditor to go through all my work.

Whew. What a relief. I had my authorial self-respect back.

I had even begun to come around to the dark little book. For whatever reason, readers liked it. The darkness resonated with people.

So, quietly, cautiously, I wrote a sequel.

This time I did it right. I took my time, knowing others would see it. I labored over word usage and plot structure. I had my beta readers and professional editors (yes, plural).

I even scheduled a blog tour and some paid advertising. Balls to the wall.

And I thought, hmm. Although sales were good and a fair amount of reviews were in for that first book, more buzz would help sales for the second book. So I went onto the BDSM Goodreads group where I had been a member for some time and made a little post saying how if anyone wanted to read the book for free, I'd be happy to give it to them. The point of this was to garner reviews, I told them, but they were in no way obligated to write a review if they accepted the book. I didn't put a limit on the number of copies because I figured not many people would even read my post, let alone request a copy.

Then something crazy happened. The very next day, the moderator sent a message blast to the group saying that my book had been selected as one of the Books of the Month for the group read and linked to my giveaway post.

I hadn't submitted my book in any way, nor had they talked to me about it beforehand. The other moderator had found my book while browsing and thought it looked interesting. They had selected as the Book of the Month before I post my giveaway and since I posted it from my other account, they didn't even know the author of that book was a member at all. It was an amazing coincidence.

Instead of the two copies I thought I'd be lucky to give out, I gave out around fifty. The moderator did reach out and let me know that I could (and maybe even should) pull the plug at any time.

Even though I have bumbled my way through a lot of this, I knew in my gut this was the right thing. Making those 50 sales was not important. Having as many people as possible participate in this group discussion of targeted readers was.

It worked. Reviews exploded for that book. Not all of them positive. In fact, that is my lowest rated book by far. The rinse of a professional copyedit could not compete with the deep cleaning of critique groups and plotting and revisions. But that month, sales topped 1000. The poor little light book was left in the dust.

The popular book hit the Amazon Erotica bestseller list, which is the gift that keeps on giving. Once it's there, it has so much more visibility. Those increased sales mean it stays on the list even longer.

And my sequel was just about ready. I released it while the first book was still on the Bestseller list, and I'm sure that helped sales. It was a bit longer and I decided to price it higher. This meant that instead of the $0.30 I received on a $0.99 sale, I made $2 per book on a $2.99 sale.

I had initially released these books to an audience of zero. Four months later, I was earning $2,500 a month.

What a ride.

Now my little-book-that-could is tiredly climbing back down the Bestseller's list. I do expect sales to take a dib after the thrill of release has died down.

However, now I know what is possible. Those three novellas combined had a lower word count than the full length novel I sold to a publisher under my old pen name. They earned enough to cover a third of my income at a fancy, high-stress tech job. They sold at night while I slept. During the day, while I played with my kid and hung out with my husband. I got a massage. Yep, still selling.

It was incredibly hard work, and yet earning the money was the easiest thing ever.

I have not reached a livable wage, but it is attainable. It's been six months now and I hope to be there within the year. Each new release will help pad that income further. Every new book will breathe sales into my previous books. Any career author will tell you that the money's in the backlist.

My little experiment turned into both a source of passive income and creative joy.

What can you learn from my amateur fumblings?

First, readers are smart as hell. They can spot the difference between a story that is written to sell and a story that fights to be told. They don't vote with their ratings but with their credit cards. When you see people complain about certain "poorly written" books topping the charts, consider that.

Though there is a market for dark stories, that isn't why they sold gangbusters. They sold because I was painfully honest, instead of tepidly trite.

Write so it hurts. Write to make yourself laugh or cry or heal. Write your way to a mindblowing orgasm. Readers didn't want my calculated, well-positioned book. They wanted my heart ripped out and served on a rusty platter.

You need to be bold, but not too bold. I didn't really believe in those novellas; they were throwaways. I did nothing to help them sell, at the beginning. About the only thing I did right was stick them up for sale. That takes some boldness.

You don't have to make the biggest splash, but you do need to get in the water.

Luck favors the prepared. And the scrappy. You saw that my assumptions were dead wrong, but it didn't matter because I tried different things and didn't give up.

In these six months that I've been self-publishing, I have seen good authors get discouraged. I have seen writers of dubious talent launch to the top of the charts. I have seen stalwart writers who have been turned down by every agent and editor *finally* find their audience and make hundreds of thousands of dollars.

It's a topsy-turvy world out here in Publishing Land, whatever path you choose.

To those of you considering taking the plunge into self-publishing, I conclude thusly: you can do better than you hope, but it will be harder than you expect.

About Skye Warren:

New York Times and *USA Today* bestselling author Skye Warren writes unapologetic erotica, including power play or erotic pain and sometimes dubious consent. There's struggle in the sex. There's pain in the relationships. Her books are raw, sexual and perversely romantic.

Website: http://www.skyewarren.com/
Email: skye@skyewarren.com
Twitter: https://twitter.com/skye_warren

11
THE SKY IS NOT FALLING, OR WHY 99-CENT BOOKS (PROBABLY) WON'T TAKE OVER THE WORLD
BY JACKIE BARBOSA

I've noticed a lot of hand-wringing over the 99-cent book. In fact, both the Huffington Post (http://www.huffingtonpost.com/karen-dionne/why-99cent-ebooks-are-a-b_b_850053.html?ir=Business) and Nathan Bransford (http://blog.nathanbransford.com/2011/04/99-cent-e-books-and-tragedy-of-commons.html) waxed eloquent on the problems with the 99 cent price point. Bransford was, in my opinion, considerably closer to the mark than the HuffPo's writer when it comes to explicating the long-term implications of the 99-cent price trend.

So, here's the thing. If you put your book up a year ago (or even 6 months ago) and priced it at 99 cents, the chances that you would move a LOT of units at that price were very high. It made sense to price in the bargain basement, even if you only made 34 cents per copy, if you could sell ten books at that price point to every one you could sell at $2.99. ($2.99 x 70% = $2.09, while $0.99 x 35% x 10 copies = $3.40).

But, as Bransford rightly notes, there's now a glut of 99-cent ebooks. There are so many, in fact, that the price point is no longer much of an enticement to readers. Yes, it's easier to get the casual browser to buy a book at 99 cents than at $2.99, but it's not as easy as it used to be. When there are so many 99-cent options to choose from, readers become pickier about what they're willing to pay even 99 cents for.

It used to be that the 99-cent price point helped browsers find you. Now, there are so many books at 99 cents, pricing at that point no longer makes your book stand out. Instead, it just leaves your book swimming in an ever-expanding pool of other books at that same price. So, unless you have something ELSE to distinguish your book from all the others (great cover art, title, concept, and most especially IMO, lots of reviews/ratings), the chances that you are going to make 10x as many sales at 99 cents as at $2.99 are simply not that great. And for the 99-cent price point to make sense financially, at least as a price for a novel-length book, you really *have to* to sell a lot more copies.

The fact that 99 cents is not a huge incentive for readers anymore was brought home to me by watching sales of my short story, THE REIVER. When I initially released it, I priced it at 99 cents (it's a very short story, so more than that seemed like price-gouging). Sales were in the neighborhood of 5-6 per day on Barnes & Noble but no more than 1 per day on Amazon. On Amazon, the book was quite simply LOST in the sea of 99 cent slush and people just weren't finding it. After a couple of months, I decided to raise the price to $1.29 on the theory that the 99 cent point wasn't bringing me any eyes I wasn't finding otherwise. Sales dropped precipitously, but then a funny thing happened. Because the Smashwords version hadn't sold but two copies, I didn't bother raising its price and Kobo (one of the retailers that gets books from Smashwords) discounted the 99-cent version to 89 cents. Amazon, being all about keeping up with the Joneses, discounted the story on their site from $1.29 to $0.89 and, lo and behold, I very quickly started selling almost 10 copies a day on Amazon.

So, are people really *that* price sensitive? We're talking a 10-cent difference between the original price and the discounted price that attracted so many more sales. What are people buying with the 10 cents they're saving? The answer, of course, is that it wasn't the prospect of saving an extra 10 cents that boosted sales–it was the fact that the 89-cent price is so unusual that by itself, it made the book stand out in a way it hadn't before. More eyes FINDING my book led to more sales.

I think the fear of a lot of authors and publishers is that 99 cents is becoming "the price" of a book, the way 99 cents has become the "price" of a song on iTunes (although, in fact, most new/popular songs are now priced at $1.29). I can understand that concern, and I've shared it to some degree, but I think in the long run, it's not going to happen because of the convergence of these three things:

1. 99 cents is no longer a point of differentiation, and…

2. The total number of books you must "differentiate" yourself from to attract readers/buyers is growing exponentially, so…

3. You will have to differentiate your book by something other than price.

It's #3 that's the sticky wicket. When 99 cents was a "marketing" point in and of itself, it made a certain amount of sense to price your book there, especially when you initially released it. But now, it's not enough (if it ever really *was*, which I doubt). Smart writers and publishers know they have a following and that the market can and will support prices of $2.99 (and more) for ebooks. The key is that, whatever the price point, your book has to be able to find its readers and vice versa. And that is going to cost authors and publishers too much for them to afford to sell their book for 99 cents indefinitely.

About Jackie Barbosa:

Jackie Barbosa is a multi-published author of historical and contemporary romance whose books have hit the top 10 in Historical Romance on both Amazon and Apple. She's been published by Cobblestone Press, Kensington Books, Harlequin and, most recently, by herself.

Reviewers have called Jackie's books "yummy and steamy as a Sally Lunn bun" and "heartfelt and sensual with a passionate spark."

Jackie took a few detours on the road, including a stint in academia (she hold an MA in Classics from the University of Chicago and was a recipient of a Mellon Fellowship in the Humanities). She learned to believe in love at first sight when she met the man of my dreams over twenty years ago and to believe in happily ever after when she married him. She lives in Southern California with her husband, their children, and an ever-changing menagerie of pets.

Jackie Barbosa wants you to stay in touch!

Website: http://www.jackiebarbosa.com
Blog: http://www.jackiebarbosa.com/blog
Twitter: http://twitter.com/jackiebarbosa
Facebook: https://www.facebook.com/jackiebarbosa
Goodreads: http://www.goodreads.com/author/show/2878436.Jackie_Barbosa
Email: Jackie@jackiebarbosa.com

12
WHY I LOVE MY CRAZY INDIE LIFE
BY DONNA MCDONALD

My writing story is similar to those of many other independent authors I know. I tried the traditional publishing route twice in my lifetime without the final success of getting published. Do I think trying the traditional route is necessary for all writers? No. Do I think I gained from it? Yes. I definitely learned about industry and the craft of my genre. It was also helpful to spend time with others trying to do what I was.

But what advice would I give to unpublished authors trying to decide which route to take? First, I would tell them that only they can make that choice. Then I would encourage them to do *something* to get their work in front of readers to gain feedback on what needs fixing. It is both arrogant and bad business to assume without validation. A writer must use strangers because ultimately "strangers" are the audience until the point of time they become readers and fans. Without a finished book, a writer is still a writer. However, with a good book people want to buy to read, a writer can become a published author making money.

I absolutely know how difficult it is to send out a query letter and a 10 page synopsis along with a partial manuscript only to be told by each of the 50 places you mailed your package to that they weren't interested in it. I also know what it's like to get close to traditional success having received a couple "fix these things and we might take another look" letters during my attempts to get published.

From August 2010 to December 2010, I spent a relatively short amount of time collecting soft rejections on two separate manuscripts. All of them began with "great story premise" or "great writing, very funny", but ended with "we just can't place your work at this time". Mostly it was because the characters in my stories tended to be older (ages 42-50) which created a niche in the contemporary romance genre where heroines are rarely over

30.

Yet these were the "stories of my heart", stories full of humor and characters who busted the hell out of the age limit on sexy. I knew how to write them and I *wanted* to write them. I was over 50 when I wrote *Dating A Cougar*. I always believed there was a giant Baby Boomer audience waiting to discover romances featuring heroes and heroines *like them*. I believed it even when it the stack of rejection letters and emails hinted differently.

Around Christmas in 2010, I had three and a half unpublished manuscripts finished and polished to the best of my ability at the time. Potential financial ruin was looming large due to a job loss in 2009 and spending most of my retirement savings the following year being a caregiver for my oldest daughter who died of cancer in June 2010. By the time I was trying to publish later that Fall, I was a mess as a grieving mother, but had a house, car, and a life with the rest of my family to try and save. Being a realist about earning a living, and yet not mentally well enough to do something "normal" everyday, I felt writing was pretty much the only thing I could do. I simply had to find a way to make it pay for me.

So with rejected manuscripts accumulating, I started asking myself some important questions. Which did I want more? Did I want a chance to be famous like my favorite authors: Nora Roberts, Janet Evanovich, and Jennifer Cruise? Or did I want to save my house and pay my bills with real money earned from my writing? Self-publishing turned out to be the only sensible, logical business choice for me, especially with books that had received mostly positive feedback from experts in the industry.

Between Christmas 2010 and January 2011, I re-evaluated my publishing goals and decided to put my funny, mature romances up for sale myself. It took from January to March to make it happen because I had a lot to learn. Frankly, I can't say enough good things about Mark Coker and Smashwords (http://www.smashwords.com), as well as Brian S. Pratt (briansprattbooks.com) (a YA author who answered my questions just because he was nice) and JA Konrath (http://jakonrath.blogspot.com/) whose revelatory blog post about the math showed me how the business part of it could work out more successfully than a traditional contract at times.

Let me just say here that I intentionally pay all the help I received forward because that is the true "secret" of Indie success, if there is one. Reciprocity is a business world view that pays off in marketing because it is the nature of most people to be nice. If you have the habit of treating people well in the rest of your life, this a literal no-brainer for your business.

I have met some amazing Indie authors, like Ruth Cardello (http://www.ruthcardello.com/books), now a *NYT* bestselling author of *Bedding the Billionaire*. Ruth wrote me in July of 2011 to tell me *Dating A Cougar* had passed her *Maid for the Billionaire* on the Amazon Top 100 free list for contemporary romances. Now she and I are cross-promo authors because her readers read my books and my readers read her books. It's been a total win-win. Ruth and I both have blogged about it. Readers can buy 3 or 4 Indie ebooks for the price of any one traditional book—and they do at small price points under $5. The only competing an Indie author really ever does is with herself to make the next book every damn bit as good as the last. Trust me—I sweat each one of mine.

Looking back on that initial effort to publish, I can honestly say that preparing a book for self-publishing wasn't any harder, or even nearly as stressful, as sending out a query, synopsis, and partial manuscript to an agent or publisher. With little guidance outside of blog posts and online articles, I made lots of mistakes self-publishing those first few books, but I also learned a ton from fixing the mistakes I made, which I still do when I find I did something wrong. I love the creative control of being an indie. I don't know if I could ever give that up.

What was the best thing I did? The money I paid per ebook cover was some of the smartest money I spent because my first series covers *still* get my work recognized over a year and half later. Before I chose to work with my cover artist, I wrote and interviewed ten. All were artistically talented and priced similarly, but I hired the one who wrote me back several times, answering all my questions very patiently. I recognized she was going to be someone I could work with well by email. I say thank-you for each one she does, pay her promptly, and make sure I let her know when someone compliments the covers on my books. I work with a separate artist to do print covers who is equally wonderful.

What was the worst mistake I made? I thought I could do all the editing myself and save that money. I was majorly wrong. Even though I had done extensive editing in my old day job, something quirky in my newly-activated creative brain caused me to see what *should be there*, not what was missing or incorrect. To this day, my #1 piece of advice to any newbie Indie author is to hire a professional editor. Hire at least the kind who will check your mechanics and find errors that spell check software can't. And no—friends and family aren't good enough. Go professional.

Hiring a professional will make your work look professional. It may even spare you some bad reviews for poor editing. I got lucky that I told a good enough story for some people to buy my second book anyway. The first money I made in May 2011 from Amazon was barely enough, but I used every penny to pay an editor to clean up Books 2 & 3 of the series. With Book 4, I was finally earning enough to allocate funds up front.

Another thing I did right was modeling my marketing after the efforts of successful Indie authors who had been selling for a while. When I put Books 1 and 2 of the *Never Too Late Series* up on March 12, 2011, I made the first book in the series, *Dating A Cougar*, completely free so readers could try my work without risk. Though a hotly debated marketing strategy, it was an easy decision for me despite the months of work I put into the writing. Why? Because in the back of my mind I feared the acquisition editors and agents were right about it not being worthy. As of February 2011, the free book had been downloaded over 350,000 times. On a personal level, the free books continues to allow readers to try my books without me taking their hard-earned cash only to disappoint them. I intend to leave it free in ebook form. The print version costs $13.99 which is the lowest I could go (based on size, etc) and still make even close to the same profit I make on a $2.99 ebook. Print is not where I make money.

You have to look at your work individually when making business decisions. In my case, sales of any one book can be small—as most niche sales are—so I knew from the beginning that I would have to have several novels selling well to make a decent living. It took around eight months of time and six published novels to see enough "real" money to pay a few regular bills. However, in the those eight months, I did more marketing and found more of my audience which early sales validated was indeed out there.

Want to know the biggest surprise I got from self-publishing? I'm having more fun than I've ever had making money. I've been a writer most of my life, but it's good to also be a "published author". I'm selling 4000-6000 books a month total in all channels consistently. Now I can't believe I ever spent time waiting for anyone in the business part of my industry to provide validation of my craft and/or permission for me to make a living from it. I could make a list of the great advice I've gotten from other Indies. Nothing is more profound than the idea that *only readers can decide if you're good enough AND that the way they do it with sales.*

Still, readers of this essay shouldn't start seeing dollar signs dancing in their heads. I describe my earnings as "modest sales" for a reason. My royalties from Amazon sales the first month on one free book and one for sale was $35, second month was $123, and the third month was only $450 *after* I put up the third book in the series. It was a long time before I saw $1000 a month. It was only recently, a year and many more books later, that I started making enough to pay most bills and feel like I could quit other work to do this full time. At the time of this essay, I have a total of 13 books published (11 for full sale + 1 free + 1 at 99 cents). It is my goal to have 17 books done by the end of 2012. I think I'm going to make it.

In a typical week day I talk to my readers via several forms of social media, and write six hours or more. On weekends I write when the story won't leave me alone. When readers ask me how many more books I intend to write, I answer that I'll keep writing for as long as they keep buying. This usually culminates with them telling me to hurry then because they're waiting for the next book.

This is the best validation any published author can hope to receive.

About Donna McDonald:

After 35 years of doing everything for a living except writing books, Donna McDonald finally published her first romance novel in March of 2011. More than a dozen novels later, she is now living her own *happily-ever-after* life as a modestly successful author who gives back to the universe by doing her best to keep several Lexington, Kentucky coffee shops in business.

In addition to writing more books, McDonald currently dreams of selling her house and taking to the open road seeking adventure, once she figures out how to do so without her children and grandchildren finding out. For the time being, she continues to live contentedly with her permanent fiancée of many years who helps her sneak away from real life as often as he can. She loves him dearly for it and thanks him for being a better hero than she could ever imagine creating for one of her books.

How to connect to Donna McDonald

Website: www.donnamcdonaldauthor.com
Contemporary Romance Blog:
http://donnamcdonald.blogspot.com/
Sci-Fi Romances Blog:
http://donnamcdonaldparanormal.blogspot.com/
Kentucky Indies Writers Blog:
http://kentuckyindiewriters.blogspot.com/
Twitter: @donnamcdonald13
(https://twitter.com/@donnamcdonald13)

Facebook: Donna Jane McDonald
(https://www.facebook.com/donnajanemcdonald)
Like Donna McDonald Contemporary Romances
(http://www.facebook.com/pages/Donna-McDonald-Contemporary-Romances/104554579626720)
Like Donna McDonald Sci-Fi Romances
(https://www.facebook.com/pages/McDonald-SciFi-Romances/104932712962609)
Pinterest: http://pinterest.com/donnamcdonald13/

13
HOW I SOLD 17,000 BOOKS IN FOUR MONTHS
BY DEBRA HOLLAND

This interview originally appeared on Shoshanna Evers' blog The Writer's Challenge.

Shoshanna Evers: If you're even thinking about self-publishing, you need to read this. Amazon bestseller and self-published romance author Debra Holland sold 17,000 books in the past four months. Yes, 17K. I interviewed her to find out as much as I could about how exactly she did that!

Thanks for being here! Can you walk us through how that happened?

Debra Holland: I can give it a try. I have some ideas, but a lot of it seems like plain good luck. :)

Much of my books' success stems from hitting two niche markets--sweet and Western. There are lots of readers out there looking for romances that are traditional. They either don't want sexy books, or they like to read both sexy and sweet.

Western romance fans tend to pounce on a Western because they don't get many of them. The historical Western market is particularly scarce.

Shoshanna Evers: Did it start slow and build or were you immediately selling well?

Debra Holland: It started slow and built, sort of like a jagged slope. I'd be at a level, then start selling a little more, stay at about that level, then bump up a bit, level out for a week or so, then go higher.

What seemed to make a difference was 5 star reviews. For each one, my sales bumped up a bit. Although, once I got to ten 5 star reviews, it didn't seem to make a difference any more.

The other thing that helped was making Amazon top 100 lists. That happened to Wild Montana Sky at about six weeks and Starry Montana Sky at about two months. The books have been climbing the lists ever since.

Shoshanna Evers: What sort of marketing did you do?

Debra Holland: I'm doing very little. Mostly I've written some personal blogs--about eight, and some guest blogs--also about eight. Not too much for four months.

I'm trying to encourage other writers to consider self-publishing. Ever since I started having success, I've been beating the self-publishing drum. I love helping others succeed. For that reason, I'm blogging very honestly about what's happening with my self-publishing career, including exact sales and money. Those blog links seemed to get passed along a lot. :)

My success isn't the norm for everyone. Many self-published authors start out far slower. But remember, sales can build over years. Think long term.

I know I should do more. I'm not even on Goodreads yet. That on my to-do list. I need to submit the books to book reviewers. Also on my to-do list. But I've trying to use my spare time to write. I think putting out new books are the best ways to promote!

Shoshanna Evers: What price points are you selling your books at, and how did you decide to sell at that price point?

Debra Holland: I'm selling Wild Montana Sky at .99 and Starry Montana Sky at 2.99. I chose .99 for the first book because I'm an unknown author, and I think readers are willing to risk trying me when the price is a bargain. I've done the same thing for the first book in my newly published Fantasy Romance series. Sower of Dreams is .99 and Reaper of Dreams is 2.99.

Shoshanna Evers: Your covers are beautiful. Who is your designer?

Debra Holland: My friend, Delle Jacobs did the Western covers. I chose a different designer, Lex Valentine, for my fantasy romances because I wanted a different look. I think all four covers are wonderful, and I'm very happy with them. Doing your own covers are definitely a benefit to self-publishing!

Shoshanna Evers: Do you have plans for future books?

Debra Holland: I'm writing the third book in the Western series, Stormy Montana Sky, and I have two more books after that. I'm hoping to have Stormy out in November. I'm also working on the third book in the Fantasy Romance trilogy, Harvest the Dreams. If I can stay on track, I'm hoping to have it out in January.

Shoshanna Evers: Do you have any suggestions for writers looking to self-publish?

Debra Holland: Learn the craft. Write a great book. Get it professionally edited. Study the market. Have FUN!

UPDATE: I sold about 120,000 books in my first 14 months, and Wild Montana Sky made the *USA Today* Bestseller list in April 2012. Amazon Montlake acquired the series, and their versions came out on August 28, 2012. Montlake will continue to publish the "big" books, and I will self-publish novellas and short stories in the series, such as Montana Sky Christmas and Painted Montana Sky.

Website: http://drdebraholland.com

14
DAVID KAZZIE, BEFORE & AFTER
BY DAVID KAZZIE

This interview from Shoshanna Evers' blog www.TheWritersChallenge.com is what we shall call "BEFORE." Wait till you see what happens AFTER. Here we go…

Shoshanna Evers: Today we have the creator of the hilarious "So You Want to Write a Novel" video answering questions for us. Here's the link to the video, in case you've been living in a wi-fi-less cabin in the woods and haven't seen it: http://youtu.be/c9fc-crEFDw

What made you create the viral Youtube video, So You Want to Write a Novel?

David Kazzie: About a year ago, I decided to take a break from writing fiction and I started writing a weekly humor blog. Because the world needed another writer's blog, right? I'd always wanted to do a humor piece about practicing law (my day job), but I couldn't come up with an angle that wasn't already tired and clichéd— making fun of lawyers is not, surprisingly, a unique subset of comedy.

Then I saw a hilarious video called iPhone 4 vs. HTC Evo, created with Xtranormal's super-easy-to-use animation website, and I thought the format would work well for a conversation between a jaded lawyer and idealistic law student. I wrote So You Want to Go to Law School one weekend and posted it to YouTube. Much to my amazement, it blew up within a few days, and it has since gotten about 1.4 million hits.

A bunch of other So You Want To… videos started popping up all over the place, but I realized around Thanksgiving that no one had done one about writing and publishing. I thought the Law School format would work well for a writing video too, so I sat down on the day before Thanksgiving, banged out the script for So You Want to Write a Novel, and sent it out on its merry way. I was really trying to roll every horror story, every misconception a new writer might have about the business into one clueless character. It caught fire over Thanksgiving weekend and started making the rounds with literary agents, editors and writers.

Shoshanna Evers: How did you get your literary agent?

David Kazzie: At its peak in early December, the Novel video was getting shared on Facebook several hundred times per hour. I stumbled across a bunch of literary agencies and authors that had posted the videos on their public Facebook pages, including the Ann Rittenberg Literary Agency. This thrilled me because Ann represents Dennis Lehane, one of my favorite writers. I left a comment thanking them for posting the video, and I didn't think much else of it at the time. A few days later Ann contacted me directly. We got to talking, and I explained who I was, what I had done, and where I planned to go with my career. We chatted off and on for the next month or so, she began reading my blog archives, and at the end of January, she offered to represent me and my career going forward. It was really unbelievable.

Shoshanna Evers: You have an agent but you just self-published your debut book. Why?

David Kazzie: I'd been monitoring the self-publishing revolution for a while, even before I wrote the videos and signed with Ann. I had a manuscript that I really believed in, even though I had reached the end of the line with querying it last year. As the months went by, the evidence that a sea change in publishing was underway was piling up, and I couldn't ignore it any longer. A couple months ago, I discussed it with Ann, and I decided that this was a perfect opportunity for me. My videos still get 1,500 to 2,000 hits per day, but I realize, the Internet being what it is, that might not last. So why not strike now, while the iron is hot with this new way of reaching readers? Starting in March, I spent every free moment I had getting The Jackpot ready. I probably worked as hard on getting it ready for publication as I did writing it in the first place.

Shoshanna Evers: Will you continue to self-publish books if you end up selling to New York?

David Kazzie: I don't know the answer to that yet. My new approach to my career is to look at everything as a business-related decision. I'm trying to build a small business here. My product is my writing, whether it's a Tweet, a blog post, an animated video, or a novel. I'll do whatever I think is best to build the business. Plus, I really trust Ann's judgment on these kinds of things, so I'm sure I'll be carefully considering the advice she gives me.

Shoshanna Evers: How has your experience with self-publishing been so far? Sales good?

David Kazzie: Like I said earlier, it was a TON of work to get the book ready for publication. I hired an editor, a cover artist, and an e-book formatter. I read my novel about eight times in 6 weeks. It was very rewarding to see the finished product, but it was exhausting. As for sales, I've tried to find statistics for other self-pubbed authors' first month or two of sales, even the ones that went one to be huge successes, and I'm happy to say that my early numbers exceed many of those. But time will tell if I can match those authors' big explosions down the road. I hope so.

Shoshanna Evers: Do you worry about the stigma self-publishing has had in the past, or do you think the stigma has disappeared now that many traditionally published authors are dipping their feet into the self-publishing waters?

David Kazzie: I thought I would worry about the stigma, but I really haven't. Like you said, so many traditionally published authors are giving it a shot. Plus, my goal is to become a full-time fiction writer, and if self-publishing opens that door for me, I for one welcome our new e-reader overlords. An author who flatly refuses to consider self-publishing as an option is really just hurting himself and ignoring the reality of what's happening in publishing.

"AFTER"

How Amazon's KDP Select Saved My Book

Gather round, my fellow writers.
I have a tale to tell.
As I write this blog post on Sunday, January 29, 2012, The Jackpot is No. 68 on Amazon's Paid Bestseller list.
(UPDATE: The book ultimately reached No. 34 on the list on January 31, 2012, and remained in the Top 100 for a total of nine days. It hung in the Top 1,000 Paid for another week or so after that.)
Cue flashback sound from Lost...
On the evening of January 24, 2012, my book was dead in the water.

And I mean dead, like a mob witness who's been taken care of. After a promising start last summer, sales crashed, completely, totally and spectacularly, despite wonderful reviews (from people who didn't even know me!). From December 1, 2011, through January 24, 2012, I sold 21 copies on Amazon. One on BN.com. And that was it. Barely enough to fund a lunch date for me and my wife. The previous couple months hadn't been much better. To be honest, I was trying to forget the book even existed as I worked on my new manuscript, my internal doomsayer wondering how badly I'd screwed my career with a self-publishing disaster.

I'd first heard about Amazon's KDP Select Program during the holidays. Here was the deal: In exchange for providing Amazon a 90-day exclusive, authors get their book(s) listed with the Lending Library, which allows Prime members to borrow books electronically. Second, authors would be able to run free promos— for each 90-day period I enroll in Select, I could make the book available for free for up to five days, divided however I liked.

At first, I wasn't sure what to think about it, especially given the exclusivity requirement. Part of me was aghast— how dare they ask me to pull my book from the other retailers! And then something occurred to me. Between October 1 and December 31, I had sold a grand total of .... ONE book on all the non-Amazon platforms— that one sale on Barnes & Noble.

I had heard anecdotal evidence that running a free promo later translated into real sales. There seemed to be no real explanation for this, other than the fact that a ton of free downloads gave a book good exposure on Amazon. So with nothing left to lose, I decided to give it a shot.

I pulled the book down from all the other e-retailers, and in the wee hours of January 25, The Jackpot went free for a two-day run. At that moment, the book had logged nine sales in January. I woke up at 6 a.m. and was surprised to see that the book had already been downloaded nearly 100 times. I knew these were downloads and not sales, but still, it was exciting to see a number other than 1 or 2 under the monthly sales tab on my Amazon report.

The download rate increased steadily during the course of the morning, and by lunchtime, it was being downloaded more than 1,000 times per hour, occasionally pushing 2,000 per hour. And it was rapidly climbing the Free bestseller list. It got featured on a number of the big Kindle reader blogs that showcase free books each day (this was easily my luckiest break, especially since I didn't know that people often submit their books to these sites in advance of their scheduled free dates). By Wednesday night, the book had hit the top 10, with about 14,000 downloads. Thursday proved to be nearly as successful, with another 11,000 downloads, and the book spent much of the day ranked No. 5.

As the day wore on, I became increasingly anxious about switching back to Paid status. What would happen? What would 25,000 free downloads mean for real sales? I was nervous.

I woke up early on Friday the 27th and checked to see what was going on. The book was back in Paid status, and it had been borrowed through the Lending Library for the first time. I noted a few sales hit as I got ready for work. This was pretty awesome, as I hadn't been sure what to expect—remember, I'd only had nine sales in January, and I was set to top that while eating breakfast. I had heard that the big sales bump for Free-to-Paid came about three days after it came off of Free status, but I didn't know how accurate that was. Regardless, I didn't want to get my hopes up on the first day.

Then sales started to pick up. It went from 225,000 to 38,000 to 10,000 on the bestseller list in short order. Then it hit No. 4,573 (the best ranking the book had ever had), and although sales continued to accelerate, its sales rank seemed to stall. I pictured the book doing mighty battle with other books in the 1,000 to 5,000 range, and I wondered if this was the Wall. Was this the place where my book would have to make its stand?

And then it broke through. It hit No. 549 by late afternoon, and No. 151 by dinnertime. It settled at No. 76 by the end of the night, and the sales kept rolling in, even late on a Friday night. It hit No. 1 among all Kindle legal thrillers, No. 2 among ALL legal thrillers (print and Kindle), and even No. 44 in Fiction and Literature, which I really like because it sounds very official.

MY THEORIES AS TO WHAT THE HELL HAPPENED

This is my guess as to how a book that couldn't muster a sale a day became an Amazon bestseller, virtually overnight.

Early Friday morning, the book continued to appear on the Free bestseller list, even though it switched back to Paid. There was a little bubble above the price marked "Why is This Not Free?", and if you scrolled over it, you got Amazon's explanation that the servers hadn't cycled out the no-longer-free books. Regardless, the now-$2.99 book was getting bestseller exposure even though it wasn't really a Paid bestseller. This only lasted for a couple of hours, but I think it helped get the ball rolling.

Also, I had so many free downloads, the book began to appear in other books' "Customer Also Bought" pages. Amazon doesn't seem to care if these books mix together on the Also-Bought lists, so many more people were seeing the book once it switched back to Paid status, even though all its prior traffic was due to free downloads. It also got a lot of exposure on the Amazon Most Popular lists (different than the bestseller lists).

Other factors that might have kept things snowballing: I write in a pretty popular genre (suspense/thrillers), and I've got a pretty cool cover.

It should be noted that several other books (from different genres) that made it to the top 10 Free List on the days I was there seem to have experienced similar success when switching to the Paid list. One book, Fresh Powder, has made it all the way to No. 26.

HERE'S THE BAD NEWS

Also worth a discussion -- what doesn't help or boost sales. I hate to say it, but I'm gonna. My blog, my Facebook fan page and Twitter feed didn't help push the book beyond the confines of my regular following.

I like blogging, so I never have done it simply as a sales tool. But any sales generated as a result of my blog posts have been minimal at best.

As for Twitter: I think I'm a decent enough Tweeter— I interact with people, I retweet interesting content, and a good number of my own tweets get retweeted. I venture outside the insulated Twitter world of writers. I like the people I interact with on Twitter and on my Facebook fan page, and those are good ways to get my blog posts out or to tell one-liner Twitter jokes (to be honest, I think Twitter is really effective for sharpening writing skills). And I don't use Twitter as a place to shill my books (I've probably sent a dozen or so self-promo Tweets, most in the days after I initially published the book).

But it's probably been ineffective as a book marketing device. Now perhaps I don't have a big enough following for it to make a difference. I know one thing— of the few hundred books I'd sold before all this happened, a good chunk were bought by my family and friends. I did very little self-promo, especially on Twitter, because I know how poorly other authors' self-promo tweets worked on me. And the tweets I did send? Probably didn't make a lick of difference. I hadn't run any advertisements, but I had purchased two (ironically, the first one didn't even run until February 27, 2012, and the second didn't run until March 31, 2012).

The thing that bummed me out the most, though, was the complete disconnect between hits on my viral animated videos and book sales. In early 2012, the videos were drawing about 1,000 hits per day -- amazing, right? But my research suggests that this translated into no more than a few dozen sales—a hundred at the very most. Why? Who knows? Maybe there isn't much overlap between Kindle readers and folks looking for a quick chuckle watching a video. I had truly believed that these videos would serve as effective billboards for me, and that people would make that jump from my YouTube page to Amazon and buy my book. Yeah. They didn't. In fact, not only did they not buy the book, very few even made the jump to my Amazon page (maybe half a dozen a day) to look at the book.

So. I'm not sure what any of this means. I learned that the Internet is a very, very noisy place, and that just about everyone is selling something. I learned that people aren't sitting around thinking about your book as much as you think and hope they are. I learned that all this time we worry about social media is probably best spent worrying about something else— like writing books.

Much like I will never quite understand why my So You Want To... videos went viral the way they did two years ago, I don't know exactly why my book finally took off the way it did. No idea how long ride this will last, but obviously, I am very thrilled and will enjoy it as long as I can.

So, if you've been thinking about trying KDP Select, I hope this gave you some additional insight into the program.

(**EDITORIAL UPDATE:** As of August 2012, it seems Amazon has changed its algorithms, making KDP Select less likely to translate free downloads into sales, but it does still offer you the chance to make your book free on Kindle, which can be amazing promo.)

About David Kazzie:

David Kazzie is a novelist and lawyer in Virginia, where he lives with his family. His debut novel, The Jackpot, reached No. 34 on the Amazon Kindle Bestseller list, and his short animated films satirizing law and publishing have been viewed more than 2 million times on YouTube.

Website: http://wahoocorner.blogspot.com
Facebook: http://www.facebook.com/SoYouWantTo
Twitter: http://twitter.com/#!/davidkazzie
Blog: http://wahoocorner.blogspot.com

15
TWITTER 101:
FIVE THINGS ABOUT TWITTER AUTHORS SHOULD KNOW (AND FIVE YOU DON'T KNOW)
BY VALERIE BOWMAN

(**Editorial Note from Shoshanna Evers:** Valerie Bowman is traditionally published author who recently self-published a <u>marketing guide for authors</u> (http://www.amazon.com/Painless-Marketing-Authors-Valerie-Bowman-ebook/dp/B00CO6QM6Y)! Her article about Twitter is extremely helpful to anyone who says they don't "get Twitter" or don't want to bother with it. If you are a self-published author, you need to be on Twitter, which is why I asked Valerie if we could share her article, originally published in the *Romance Writer's Report*. Read on!)

Ah, Twitter. The social media highway. That fast-paced metropolis of keystrokes answering the age-old question…What are you doing? Whether you love it or hate it, it's there, running at top speed 24/7 and offering up some of the best info in the industry if you know how to find it.

I hear a lot of people say they don't 'get' Twitter. And granted, it can be a bit overwhelming. So, here are a few things you should know, a few things you may not know, and a few just-for-fun tips. A romance author's guide to the Twittersphere.

First things first. If you are new to Twitter and have no (or little) idea how it works, I recommend Jessica Hische's easy-to-read article on the subject: *This is How Twitter Works, Mom.* (Sorry, her title, not mine!) You can find it at: <u>http://www.jhische.com/twitter/</u>.

Now, at the risk of repeating a lot of oft-used Twitter advice, here are the five things you should *probably* already know. But don't worry, there's plenty of time to catch up. Read on!

On Twitter…

Do NOT pitch to editors or agents, spam, retweet constantly, or follow people, wait for them to follow you back, and then unfollow them. These are all seriously uncool Twitter behaviors. For more of these little tidbits, check out author Dee Carney's (@dee_carney) fantastic list of Twitter Dos and Donts on her website at

http://www.deecarney.com/2010/07/22/why-i-stopped-following-you/.

Make sure you've got an actual picture (preferably of yourself) attached to your account (that default egg is no good). Also ensure that your bio is up-to-date and isn't just a mention of your latest book. I see so many authors who don't include anything personal about themselves in their bio. The best bios (in my humble opinion) give you a brief glimpse into the mind of the writer, an idea of who they are as a person in addition to the title of their book.

If all you're doing is tweeting "buy my book" or "buy my friend's book" step away from Twitter. You're doing it wrong. I think some people have heard this advice so much, they're listening, but they still don't GET it. Last week, I had a guy tweet me in response to something personal I posted. That was nice. Five minutes later, he sent me a "check out my website/buy my book" link. Uh, one tweet does not a relationship make. As author Ashlyn Macnamara (@ashlyn_mac), A MOST SCANDALOUS PROPOSAL, puts it, "Don't DM (direct message) me a link to your book/blog/whatever the second you've noticed I followed you (or ever, even)." Relax. Hang out. Make friends. And seriously, don't ask me (or anyone) to retweet a link to buy your book unless I actually KNOW you. Uncool.

If you can help it, don't put a number or an underscore in your twitter name (research shows those with a number or an underscore have less followers). It's also seriously difficult to find the underscore key on an iPhone and believe me, a lot of people, yours truly included, use Twitter almost solely from a smart phone. Also, don't use a cutesy name like @writergirl85. I know. A lot of you with pre-established Twitter names are groaning. "But I'm already @ILOVEROMBKS," you're saying. I learned this name tidbit from Kristen Lamb (@KristenLambTX) in her great book about social media, *We Are Not Alone*. As an author, you should be branding yourself…your name or your pseudonym, whatever name your books will be for sale under. If a reader/buyer is going to the web or into a bookstore to find your book, they aren't going to search/ask for writergirl85. They need your last name. They should have it! The good news is you can change your handle with relatively little trouble. If you do, be sure to change it anywhere you have your Twitter name posted.

"My tip?" asks author Jennifer Delamere (@jendelamere) AN HEIRESS AT HEART, (https://www.facebook.com/jennifer.d.harrington) "Sometimes you have to Step. Away. From. The Internet. If you are tweeting as an author, consider your audience. When controversial issues arise, your readers may not agree with your opinion, and they may not even want to hear it. Don't lose readers who love your books simply because you spoke (or tweeted, or even re-tweeted someone else) in haste." She's absolutely right! It can be tempting to jump into the fray, Twitter is very fast and easy once you get going but take a second to think about it. Really. Trust me. You'll thank me later.

All right, so those are the things you often hear about Twitter, what are the five things you don't (or may not) know?
How to get 2,000+ followers. You want to know how to get over 2,000 Twitter followers? It's easy. Start following people! A really smart way to do it is to follow the followers of an author who writes like you. If you think her followers would enjoy your type of books, follow them and see if they follow you back. Do NOT, however, harass them with messages touting your book or even comparing it to said author's work. Bad idea! Just follow. Twitter is a social environment. Keep it social. Use a service like www.Tweepi.com (which is free for the basic service) to flush anyone who's not following you back and to follow those who are following you. If you only follow industry executives and New York Times best-selling authors, odds are, they won't follow you back and your numbers will be skewed. Follow regular everyday Janes and be friendly, not pushy.

Join a tribe but don't spam people with it. You may have heard of Triberr (www.Triberr.com) but you may not know what it is exactly. Triberr is a twitter reach multiplier and it can do amazing things! You basically get together with other people who tweet the same sort of information you do (I belong to a Regency writers tribe, for example) and then you retweet for each other. I'm not going to sugar coat it, Triberr has a few— shall we say?—bugs, but my reach on Twitter went from around 2,000 to around 22,0000 when I joined two tribes. Well worth a few kinks. Note that some people think Triberr is a big, old spam service and there is certainly an argument to be made for that, so if you're going to use it, be extremely judicious in your retweets from Triberr and time them so they don't all go out at once.

You should be using Twitter to stalk industry big wigs. Ok, *stalk* may be the wrong term. But I'll tell you, before I got my first contract when I was out on submission, I used Twitter to see what my agent and potential editors were up to. If you're dying to hear back on a submission, Twitter can tell you that particular editor is out of town for two weeks. Agents and editors are also constantly tweeting about what they're looking for in the slush piles, what they aren't looking for, and giving great and useful feedback on queries and such. Agents Kevan Lyon (@KevanLyon) and Sara Megibow (@SaraMegibow) regularly do a 10 Queries in 10 Tweets feature where they post their reactions to queries in real-time. And if you search Twitter for #pubtip or #askagent you'll see a ton of useful info. You can get to know a bit about the personality and work style of the agents and editors you're querying. No, not all of them are on Twitter, but you may be surprised how many of them are.

You're NOT *supposed* to read everything. Twitter is like popping into an online cocktail party. You're only going to hear the conversation you're paying attention to at the moment. It's not meant to be something you keep dibs on 24/7. Writer Carla Kempert (@CarlaKempert) says, "Don't make yourself crazy trying to keep up with everything posted on Twitter (the way you can with Facebook). That way lies madness. You can't keep up with the volume, it's impossible, so don't even try."

How to search all that content. One of the best ways to search Twitter is by using Topsy, http://topsy.com/advanced-search. To find people talking about you or your books or other topics in the field, use http://twitter.com/#!/search-home.

So, hopefully you've learned something new, but just for the fun o' it, here are five extra Twitter tidbits to consider. I asked my tweeps for advice and they delivered!

Scheduled Tweets:
Author Sheila Athens (@SheilaAthens) advises, "Schedule tweets via TweetDeck so you have presence while at day job." You can also do this using Twuffer.com and a variety of other applications that connect with Twitter.

Don't confuse your Tweeps
Author Rowena May O'Sullivan (https://www.facebook.com/rowenamayo) (@RowenaMayo) says, "Don't assume everyone knows what you mean!" This is good advice. You and your friends may have inside jokes on Twitter but unless you are DM'ing back and forth and keeping your conversation private, you may be confusing the heck out of your other followers.

Watch out for spam links.
Yes, Twitter is as susceptible as anything else on the internet when it comes to spammers, phishers, and the like. Author, Kathryn Jane (https://www.facebook.com/kathryn.jane.921) (@Author_Kat_Jane) says, "Be careful of a message that says something like, 'Look at this great picture of you.' or 'Is this you?' etc. If you open the link attached it will be a virus or compromise your security somehow." Another popular fake link is, "Check out what someone is saying about you!" Don't fall for it.

MT means modified tweet i.e., the person who retweeted it has changed it somehow (usually to shorten it). RT means retweet. A period in front of an exchange means that all followers can see it, not just those named in the tweet.

Use hashtags.
If a word has # in front of it, it's a hashtag. Hashtags are keywords that help you reach a specific audience. Use them to find content to read or to direct others to your content. For example, if you wanted to check out all the tweets streaming from the RWA 2012 Conference, the hashtag was #RWA12. If you were tweeting from the conference, you would put #RWA12 at the end of your tweets so people looking for conference tweets could find yours. Tweets that include hashtags receive twice as much engagement than those without. Source:
http://community.constantcontact.com/t5/Social-Media/What-you-need-to-know-about-Twitter-hashtags/m-p/59769

But Does Twitter Actually Sell Books?
At the PASIC (Published Authors Special Interest Chapter) conference in New York in March, there was a lot of discussion about whether social media actually sells books. The RWA reader survey presented by Bowker lends credence to the fact that very few readers are actually on social media and making buying decisions because of it. I know. I know. For every author who says she's never once sold a book via Twitter, I'll get an email from five more who say they make sales that way every day. I really do think it depends on the author and her personal audience.

I've been on Twitter for years and here's how I look at it. Twitter is like the authors' water cooler. You can pop on, see what's up, congratulate your coworkers, say hello, keep track on what editors or agents may be looking for, or talking about. Then, go back to work. If someone sees you on there and buys your book as a result, all the better. A nice side-effect of spending time out there. Personally, I don't use Twitter for sales. I'm out there because I like being part of the conversation and yes, I'm a sucker for the occasional people-watching stream. So, I say, treat Twitter like a social atmosphere and the benefits, if any, will follow.

Happy Tweeting!

About Valerie Bowman:

Award-winning author and Golden Heart® finalist, Valerie Bowman, writes Racy Regency Romps with a focus on sharp dialogue, engaging storylines, and heroines who take matters into their own hands! She's published with St. Martin's Press. **Publishers Weekly** calls Secrets of a Wedding Night, an *"enchanting, engaging debut that will have readers seeking future installments"* and **Romantic Times Book Reviews** says, *"This fast-paced, charming debut, sparkling with witty dialogue and engaging characters, marks Bowman* *for stardom."* **Booklist** gave it a starred review!

Valerie has a degree in English Language and Literature from Smith College and lives in Jacksonville, FL with her rascally dog, Roo. When she's not writing, she keeps busy reading, traveling, or watching either PBS or reality TV.

Valerie Bowman wants you to stay in touch!

Website: www.ValerieBowmanBooks.com
Blog: www.DashingDuchesses.com
Twitter: www.Twitter.com/ValerieGBowman
Facebook: https://www.facebook.com/ValerieBowmanAuthor
Goodreads: http://www.goodreads.com/Valerie_Bowman
Email: valerie@valeriebowmanbooks.com

16
MARKETING BY THE EBOOK
BY K. ROWE

As authors, most of us detest the "M" word. I'm no exception. But, if you play your cards right, marketing opportunities can literally fall in your lap- FREE ones at that!

So, now you're wondering what stupendous things I'm going to tell you. This works very well if you're a prolific author. The reason being, the tactic is to draw folks to you, and your hopefully healthy backcatalog. This is pretty much a no-cost option to getting ebooks in people's hands. And you know what? I didn't think this up. I owe all the credit to one of my Indie author peers. He suggested this to me, simply because it worked for him—so well, he finally got to quit his day job and become a writer full time. How did he do it? He wrote a "free" ebook.

By free, he explained to me that I was to write either a novella or a full length novel. Even better, make it the first book in a series to get readers hooked and wanting more. Once completed, I got beta readers to go over it, and made any corrections. Since I have the know-how, I formatted and did the cover—all for little to no cost. The less money I put into it, the better. It didn't mean I was to cut corners, no, that book had probably 12 editing passes by me. Was it perfect? No! In fact I've had to make corrections and upload new versions. But I did the best I could for the lack of money.

Once you have this free ebook done, now you need to get it up on the internet for the entire world to see. This is where it can get a little tricky. We all know Amazon is the best place to get exposure. BUT, they won't let you put a book up there for free (unless you do the KDP Select with it). So, how do you get Amazon to price your book for free if you don't want to do Select? It requires a little patience, but in the end, it's worth it.

First: publish the book on Smashwords.com. You can list it there for free. Cool, tell folks about it. Smashwords isn't as well known and the mighty Amazon, but, they also have a deal with Amazon that involves price matching. So, once your book is showing up free on Smashwords, go to Amazon and publish there (just slap a .99 price on it for now) then get your friends, fellow authors, whomever, to log onto Amazon and use the price matching feature. They will need the link to your book for both sites. It took me just over a month and Amazon dropped the price to free.

Second: the media blitz. Facebook is a wealth of information, if you know where to look—or like me, just have dumb luck and stumble upon it. I started noticing my "friends" showing links to eReader News Daily and Pixel of Ink. Both are sites that post free Kindle books on a daily basis. I went to the eReader News website, found a contact email, and sent them a very polite email letting them know I had a free ebook on Amazon (and it was totally free, not KDP Select) and gave them the link. They sent me a nice email back and informed me of the day they would post my book (it was a Friday, I think). Up until now, my book had seen good movement in the free sci-fi-adventure category on Amazon but nothing fantastic. After eReader News posted that link, I could sit and watch my downloads going up by the very minute! I had over 1,000 downloads in ONE DAY!!! I was absolutely amazed! At the peak of the downloading frenzy, my book was #4 on the list.

Third: don't sit back on your laurels. Yes, I had a top 10 "bestseller" on my hands, but that didn't mean I stopped. I used Twitter, and finally figured out how those hashtags worked. By using #free #ebook #Kindle #sci-fi in my tweets, folks searching those words might stumble over my link for the book. It must've worked; I've picked up quite a few new followers on Twitter. Which leads me to:

Fourth: steering them to you! We're all just minnows in this giant sea of publishing. So how do you get someone to find you? Well, simple: tell them! When posting on Facebook or Twitter, don't be afraid to insert your Amazon author page link. Yes, you're tooting your own horn, but in case you haven't noticed, no one else is there to do it for you. And make sure that page is as compelling as you can get it. Have the best picture you can of yourself, a bio that's interesting, perhaps a bit funny, and engages your audience to want to know more about you and your books. Basically, you're pimping yourself.

Okay, so now you've done all this, what to expect? I have the book posted on Smashwords, Amazon, and Barnes and Noble—all for free. What I've seen is a gradual increase in my backcatalog sales—especially on Amazon. The free ebook is still getting downloads (it has fallen in the ranking but is still in the top 100) and now folks have hopefully read their free sample and are looking at what else I have to offer; or looking forward to part two.

Now, what next? More marketing! What? What? You say? **More??!!**

Yes, this is the easiest of all. When you are formatting your books, don't forget to either put in the front or back matter any links you have: website, Facebook page, Twitter handle, anyway you would want your adoring fans to have access to you. ---A word of caution: DO NOT put your Amazon author page, or your Smashwords author page—you will run into problems with conflicts of interest between the sellers and they may dump your book. Just use non-company related sites. If the book is part one of a series, don't forget to put: "Watch for Part 2 of _____" so they know there is more to come. And list any of your backcatalog along with your bio at the end, so they know you offer something else to read.

This strategy worked well for me. Will it work for you? You never know until you try. There are so many ways to get your book out there, but for many of us, we can't afford to fork out loads of dough for advertising. So use what's freely available and make it work. Don't be afraid to be creative—we're writers for Pete's sake—we're supposed to be creative!

Here are some helpful links:
http://ereadernewstoday.com/
http://www.pixelofink.com/
https://authorcentral.amazon.com/

About K. Rowe:

K. Rowe is an award winning, best-selling, multi-genre author who writes under Sturgeon Creek Publishing. Her genres include: military thrillers, romance, sci-fi, and erotica; with many more stories of various genres on the way. Her novella, "Cowboys and Olympians" was a Smashwords bestseller. "Project: Dragonslayers," was a Military Writers Society of America award winner.

She's a 100% Indie published author; using Amazon, Barnes and Noble, and Smashwords for eBooks; and CreateSpace for print. One reviewer wrote: "Watch out Tom Clancy!"

Rowe has her own tractor- a 1953 Ferguson TO-30, and lives on a 100 acre mostly organic farm in eastern Kentucky.

K. Rowe wants you to stay in touch!

Blog: http://sturgeoncreek.blogspot.com/
Twitter: @Sturgeon3736
Facebook: http://www.facebook.com/K.RoweAuthor
http://www.facebook.com/ProjectDragonslayers
Email: sturgeon3736@yahoo.com

17
THE WORLD OF A STEAMPUNK INDIE
BY HEATHER HIESTAND/ANH LEOD

In late summer 2011, I had a completed steampunk novel for which I had turned down representation, due to the heinous nature of the agent's contract. It was sitting on the desk of various editors in New York, as it had been for some time. To be honest, at the time of the writing of this essay, it is still on those same editors' desks. I was frustrated again by my efforts to expand my career from small press to major publishers.

I had a great idea for a Christmas-themed steampunk novel, which I thought I should write to build my credibility as a steampunk author, but knew my regular publishers required too much lead time to release the story by Christmas. Since I didn't know how long steampunk was going to be viable, I wanted to get my story out in 2011. This is why I chose to go indie. Eventually, a new author friend suggested I try her publisher since they had a shorter timeframe to release and my story exactly fit their guidelines, but I had already purchased my cover so I stayed on the indie path. Things might have been different if I wasn't friends with a cover artist who was inspired by the etching I found.

This, my first Heather Hiestand indie release, *Captain Andrew's Flying Christmas*, came out in mid October 2011, after multiple drafts, several critiques and beta reads, and a proofread by a professional copy editor. It immediately caught the imagination of other steampunk-inclined authors, partially because the cover was eye-catching. Any success this story had is due to other writers, from a steampunk class, an indie author and promotion loop, the ninety-nine cent indie book blowout sale that came out of those loops, and my writer network. I quickly sold past my expectations, based on my recent small press experiences.

At this date, I have nine reviews on Amazon for it, all five stars, which amazes me. The novella reached bestseller status in early December for one day, on the Romance Anthology list. I do know most of the people who have reviewed the story. Reviews are so important these days. You need them to advertise on some of the most active promotion sites, for instance, and books tend to sell better when reviews are present.

(Editorial Update: As of this writing (November 2012) Amazon has been removing some reviews written by authors that they feel violate their Terms, despite the fact that writers are among the most prolific readers. It makes sense that we'd want to leave reviews for good books to help spread the word. Karma, right?)

I've had a couple of surprises along the way. This story is clearly branded as a Christmas story, but it is still selling. Not as well as it did before the holidays, but it's never stopped selling entirely. The second surprise is the death of my expectation that the second story in this series would do as well as the first. I expected the series to build, especially since feedback was so positive with the first story. Unfortunately, *Captain Fenna's Dirigible Valentine* has not reached bestseller status.

Why? Covers are vitally important to indie authors. They create appeal. We have to be ready to make changes when they aren't selling our work for us. I believe the cover of my second novella appeals to too narrow an audience. Additionally, I believe my readership has mostly been authors. I need to broaden my readership. I chose a subgenre that romance readers seem to be a bit scared of. I didn't know this when I published. Indie publishing is a great way to get the book of your heart out, but you can't expect everyone to love the esoteric stuff that you do. On the other hand, subgenres that mass market publishers consider dead (like romantic suspense and time travel at the time of this writing) can do very, very well in indie publishing.

For what it is, a narrowly focused novella, I think *Captain Andrew's Flying Christmas* has been very successful.

For my third journey into indie publication, I turned to my alter ego, erotic romance author Anh Leod, and published *Clockwork Captive*. My expectations for a solo erotic romance novella release were more modest than if I'd submitted and sold the story to one of my publishers, but since steampunk is a DIY kind of phenomenon, I wanted to stay indie for this story. Did I meet my modest expectations? Yes, after a rocky first few weeks.

Pricing is a tricky area in publishing. I chose a price point that was lower than what my publishers would charge, but would pay me the same royalty. Initially, I wasn't finding many buyers, so I put the story on sale for a time. More importantly than that, I made the story FREE.

Yes, FREE is a huge marketing tool right now for indie publishing. It's not as powerful as it was in 2010, but it still increases DISCOVERABILITY. How does anyone find your story to buy it? They can't purchase what they can't find. I had hoped my erotic romance name was big enough to create discoverability, along with my network of people who could "like and tag" the story for me, and those first reviews, again mostly by people I knew. But the price point defeated me, along with an unwieldy blurb and cover.

Yes, my main marketing tools defeated me too. My blurb—too long. My cover—not sensual enough. I took my concerns to the readers on a review website loop, and this is what they told me. Feedback is critical. Form your own market analysis team! Once I changed the blurb, cover, price, and made the story free for two days, I had both discoverability and desirability, and my sales have met my expectations.

How do I define discoverability? It's not just your website, newsletter, blog, tweets, Facebook or presence on promotional loops or websites, paid or unpaid. It is being on the pages of other author's books (or your own) in those "also-bought" lists on bookstore websites. Even better, it is hitting their bestseller lists, which is often self-perpetuating.

I still plan to tweak all three of my indie releases over time. Since I'm the publisher, nothing is set in stone. Authors no longer have to sigh over sad publisher-made covers and copy and let those stories drop like a stone. We have the power to allow our stories to be seen in the ever-changing marketplace.

This power is what makes indie publication so attractive. For writers like me, who are accomplished enough to sell just about everything they write, but not necessarily to call any of the shots or be financially successful, indie publication is a wonderful new tool. I think it is a dangerous way to go if the market (or at least writing contests) hasn't told you that you are publishing-ready. You are still putting your work in front of an audience and you need to put your best product out there. Be ready, be nimble, be excited!

About Heather Hiestand:

Heather Hiestand is the author of many novels, novellas and short stories and has been published since 2005. She is an Amazon Romance Anthology Bestseller and Amazon UK Romance Short Stories Bestseller. She lives in Washington with her husband and son. She also writes as Anh Leod. Find Heather Hiestand online:

Website: http://www.heatherhiestand.com
Blog: http://blog.heatherhiestand.com
Twitter: http://twitter.com/#!/hahiestand
Facebook: http://www.facebook.com/pages/Heather-HiestandAnh-Leod/24271017921?ref=ts

18
GETTING PUBLISHED
BY SHOSHANNA EVERS

This essay was originally published in How to Write Hot Sex (a #1 Bestseller in the Authorship, Erotic Writing, and Romance Writing categories!). But since in this essay I wrote about the business aspect of publishing instead of about sex, I figured you might find this information helpful, whether you're a newbie to the world of publishing, a traditionally published author looking to self-publish, or a self-published author looking to get into traditional publishing.

I'll assume you've got your craft in order—that by now, you've got the knowledge to write a spectacular manuscript. Then what? This essay tells you where to go after you've written the words "The End."

There are a variety of options available, but they won't all be right for you, or for a particular story. I'm going to break down exactly how getting traditionally published works, and how self-publishing works. Both are viable options.

Many of you reading this book are already experienced in the art of writing query letters. You know all of the Big 6 publishers (**Editorial Update:** As of November 2012 we've got the Big 5, since Random House and Penguin merged. I was hoping they'd call it Random Penguin, but they've called it Penguin Random House. Oh well.) and you've got your hearts set on a particular agent (or you're bypassing this route to go indie first).

But others may not know, so I'm going to start at the beginning, and please forgive me if you think I'm being obvious. It didn't occur to me to write about the basics first until I spoke with a friend who was interested in writing as well. As we spoke, it became clear she didn't know the difference between an agent, and editor, and a publisher. Or the difference between a NY publisher, an e-publisher, vanity publishing, and self-publishing. So I'll go through some basic terms you'll hear bandied about a lot in publishing circles.

Oh wait, you're not in any circles? Let's get you connected really quickly then. Join Twitter. Don't tell me you don't "get" Twitter. Simply put, if you are an author or are aspiring to be one, you are shooting yourself in the foot by avoiding Twitter. You don't need to have a fancy phone or be able to text (myths that kept me off Twitter for years). Just go online to www.Twitter.com and use your pen name as your Twitter handle. That way you're building name recognition every time you Tweet. I like to use TweetDeck, a free software that makes Twitter really easy to use. You can set up searches for hashtags, which are topics. On TweetDeck, I create a separate column for each of my favorite hashtags: #amwriting #amediting #amreading #askeditor #askagent #writechat and #pubwrite. Just like that, you've found other writers and authors and publishing peeps online to connect with.

Also, one thing I've heard over and over again is "I tried Twitter, but I have nothing interesting to say." No! You've got it all wrong. Twitter isn't about shouting into the Universe, it's about listening. Follow anyone you like. Follow Publisher's Weekly. Follow all the big literary agents. Follow your favorite authors—and tell them they're your favorite! We love that. Really really truly. Unlike another author who shall remain nameless, I will never complain about getting too much fan mail, LOL. When a reader reaches out to me, I literally save their email to re-read when I need a pick-me-up.

Sorry, we got off track. Where were we? Oh yes, getting yourself into some writing circles and getting into the community. The publishing world is small. We all know each other. We've all heard of each other, at least. With that in mind, try not to start drama. Don't put down anyone or talk smack. Things have a way of getting around—and words live on the internet forever. I once wrote a blog post back in 2009 saying I thought self-publishing was the worst thing an author could do to her career. In 2011, with four other publishers under my belt, I self-published and became an Amazon bestseller (and in 2014, a *New York Times* and *USA Today* Bestseller with a self-published project, as well). I make real money with my self-published titles. But if you Google back far enough, my name is attached to an essay that is hopelessly outdated. *shrugs* At least I always knew better than to badmouth people! I don't even give bad reviews. If you look on Goodreads (oh hey, join Goodreads) you'll see I only give 5 star reviews. If I can't give a book 5 stars, I won't review it. As far as I'm concerned, if I said something bad about a book, I'm saying something to the author, to her agent, to her editor, to all of the readers who loved it, etcetera. I'm not in this business to start shit. I'm here to write. That's not a value judgment on you if you choose to go around giving books 1 star reviews, because everyone has the right to express their opinion. It's just how I choose to conduct myself online. That's how I roll, baby!

Speaking of expressing opinions, there are some great author forums online, such as Absolute Write, where you can find tons of information. Start by lurking and getting a feel for the forum and the etiquette. I've got a blog at www.TheWritersChallenge.com, and I have years of searchable publishing advice and author interviews to sift through, along with the actual challenge: to write 1000 words a day, every day. Don't be one of those non-writing writers. A Harlequin author once told me her success is based on BICHOK: Butt In Chair, Hands On Keyboard. That's some damn good advice right there.

Wait a minute, wasn't I about to introduce you to some important publishing terms? Here we go, in alphabetical order:

Advance: Money a publisher pays you upfront for your manuscript to be published. After you earn out your advance, you get royalties, ie more money. The average advance for a first novel is $5000. I've heard that only 1 out of 5 published books earns out its advance and starts making royalties. Most e-publishers, by the way, either don't pay advances or pay very tiny advances ($100-$200). They make up for it by paying you royalties right away. Want to know real figures about what publishers are actually paying out in terms of advances, royalties, and total earn-out? Check out Brenda Hiatt's Show Me the Money (http://brendahiatt.com/show-me-the-money/).

Agent: a literary agent works on commission. You query them about your (completed) manuscript, and hope like hell they eventually get back to you with a request to see pages. If they love your book enough, they'll shop it around to New York (that is, the big publishing houses) and try to get an editor at one of the houses interested in buying your book. If they make the sale, the agent gets 15% of your advance and royalties for shopping it and negotiating your contract. You can't get into most of the big houses without an agent, and even if you did, you'll still need an agent to negotiate on your behalf so you don't accidentally option your firstborn son, LOL

Beta-reader: someone who reads your manuscript before you send it out into the big bad world. Someone who is not your mom or your husband. A beta-reader can provide valuable insight into what works and what doesn't work. I like to use a variety of beta-readers, listen to everything they have to say, and make changes as needed. If everyone says they didn't understand something or they hate another thing, I'll listen. But if one person loves it and the other hates it, then tie goes to the author, as Stephen King says. Oh hey, read *On Writing* by Stephen King. It may not be about hot sex, but it is fabulous.

Critique-partner: a CP is like a beta-reader but more in-depth. Usually a CP is another author, someone whose opinion you trust. You send your manuscript to your CP and make changes before sending it to any beta-readers.

Editor: this is the person your agent has lunch with so she can pitch your manuscript to the editor, and then the editor buys your book (um, hopefully) and works with you on edits. An editor can also be someone you hire to polish a manuscript before self-publishing. Usually an editor focuses on big-pictures stuff, saving typos and minor grammatical or continuity issues for the copyeditor. This is *not* an excuse to slack off on writing the best book you can. If your manuscript gets submitted to an editor looking like it actually needs editing, it won't be acquired. That's because the editor has a hundred, hell, a thousand other manuscripts sitting on her desk that are ready to go.

E-publisher: Ellora's Cave, Samhain, Carina Press, Avon Impulse, Entangled, The Wild Rose Press, Loose Id, Ravenous Romance, Red Sage, Total-e-Bound, I could go on and on because there's a lot, with new ones cropping up each day. They mainly produce ebooks, although they'll also sell trade paperbacks using POD (print on demand). E-publishers acquire manuscripts, edit them, create the cover art, format them, and upload them for the author, and then pay the author royalties on the book sales. Most e-pubs pay between 25-40% royalties and no advance. Don't confuse e-publishing with self-publishing. E-publishers are similar to traditional publishers in the sense that you have a less-than-stellar shot at getting published with them due to the massive amount of queries they receive, and they have to make a time and money investment in your book that they feel will make them money.

E-reader: a device to read ebooks on. If you don't have an ereader, you can still read ebooks on your computer by downloading free ereading software such as the Kindle or Nook app, or Adobe.

KDP: Kindle Direct Publishing. This is where self-publishers go to make some serious money. Or, to sell 4 books a month (the oft-quoted average for self-pubbed authors). Whichever. Anyone can write something and upload it to the Amazon Kindle store for free using KDP. *Anyone.* Which means there's a lot of crap out there, but there's a lot of amazing books too. I've come to the point where I don't care if a book is self-published, NY published, or pubbed by one of the e-publishers. All I care is if the cover and blurb are great. If they are, I download a free sample, and if I'm hooked by the end of the sample…I can buy it with one click and be reading it in under sixty seconds. Score!

Kindle: Amazon's Kindle is my personal ereader of choice because I prefer the Amazon bookstore, although everyone has their own favorite. Kindles are an easy way to download books. My husband didn't want a Kindle because he said he didn't read enough to justify the cost. I bought him one anyway, and guess what? He carries it with him everywhere and reads all the time now. Having access to a 24/7 bookstore is heaven.

Nook: Barnes & Noble Nook is different from the Kindle in that it has color and has a touch screen. In my experience, the Nook readership has different buying habits than the Kindle readership. On Kindle, my 99 cent book sells better than my more expensive books (**2014 update:** Now my higher priced books at $4.95 sell better. Change in algorithms?). On Nook, the opposite is true—but overall sales on Nook are less than on Kindle. Way less. Not sure why, all I know is if you have an ebook, you want it on both Kindle and Nook. There are other ereaders in town, of course. Sony, Kobo, others I can't think of. But in terms of publishing platforms, I focus on Kindle and Nook and let Smashwords distribute to the others.

Nook Press: this is Barnes & Noble's publishing platform, similar to Amazon Kindle's KDP.

NY publisher: I'd never heard this term until after I sold my erotic short *The Wooden Pony* to Berkley Heat (an imprint of Penguin, one of the Big 6 (...Big 5, whatever. Mergers make a term we've bandied about for ages—ie The Big 6—obsolete.) for the Agony/Ecstasy anthology. I was at the Ellora's Cave Romanticon convention in Ohio when I found out. One of the other authors said, "Wow, now you're NY published!" Apparently this is a big deal. I had not been aware of that. Basically, in many people's minds, you're "really" published if NY wants you. At this point I think you're "really" published if people pay money for your books, however those books got there. My self-pubbed ebooks are distributed on the same page as my traditionally pubbed books and guess which I make more money with? Weird, huh. Still, I can't help but love the idea of NY, and that's why I have an agent and give her manuscripts in addition to publishing with my e-publishers and self-publishing as well. (**Editorial update:** Speaking of NY publishing, as of this writing (in 2012) I recently signed a six-book deal with Simon & Schuster, with the understanding that I could continue to self-publish. It will be interesting to see how this plays out. I'm hoping to reach a broader audience through them; we'll see! Fingers crossed!) (**Another Editorial Update**: Now (November 2012) there's talk of the possibility of HarperCollins and Simon & Schuster merging?! If that happens, we'll be down to the Big 4, I suppose.) (**2014 Update** - that hasn't happened yet. We're still at the Big 5).

POD: print on demand. This is how e-pubs sell print books. They don't do a huge print run and then pulp all the books that don't sell, like NY does. They create the book file, and every time a customer orders one, it gets printed (on demand!). If you self-publish, you can also offer your book in print using POD. For the love of all things holy, don't go to a vanity publisher and have tons of overpriced books printed up. You'll spend thousands and end up with a basement full of moldy books. I know several people who've done this (and by the way, this is what I used to think "self-publishing" meant).

PubIt: this is what Barnes & Noble's publishing platform, similar to Amazon Kindle's KDP, used to be called, before they rebranded it **Nook Press.** Some authors still call Nook Press "PubIt" out of habit.

Publisher: the publisher is the person or company who distributes digital or printed books. Publishers are the intermediary between the author and the reader. Unless you self-publish, in which case you, the author, is the publisher. Publishers hire editors who acquire manuscripts.

Query: a query letter is a one page business letter (or email, nowadays) that tells the agent or editor what your book is about in a paragraph or two, and then a paragraph about your writing experience. If you have no experience, you can mention any writing classes you've taken or associations you belong to, such as Romance Writers of America. Query letters are an art. If the query sucks—or rather, if the query isn't perfect—you can kiss your chances of an agent or editor requesting pages goodbye. How to write a query letter could be its own entire essay. In fact, if you Google that phrase you'll find a ton of advice. Just remember this: don't dash off a quick email with your manuscript attached and expect results. Take your time. Have beta-readers read your query. This is your first introduction to an agent or editor, and you want it to be flawless.

Royalties: the percentage of book sales the author gets paid. It's really low on print books, often like 6 or 7%. Higher on e-pubbed books: 25-40% usually. If you self-publish, you get 70% if your book is priced between $2.99 and $9.99 on Kindle, or 35% if it's priced higher or lower. One thing to consider is you'll need to sell six times more books at the 99 cent price-point than you will at the $2.99 price point in order to make the same amount of money.

Self-publishing: when the author is the publisher. You take your own book, and do everything the publisher would normally do for you all by yourself (or farm it out for hire). You have someone that's not you edit your manuscript, and then you take care of (or pay a flat fee for help with) formatting, cover design, and uploading it to distribution outlets like Amazon Kindle, Smashwords, Apple, Kobo, and Barnes & Noble Nook.

Smashwords: a distribution website that puts out your books in all formats. Readers can buy your book from Smashwords directly, and Smashwords also distributes your book to all the outlets for you.

The Big 5: (See all my little editorial updates under NY Publisher. The giants are merging and so it's not quite the Big 6 anymore.) The big six huge NY publishers have hundreds of imprints. Hachette Book Group is known mainly for its imprints Grand Central and Little, Brown and Co; HarperCollins (Avon); MacMillan Publishers (Tor and St. Martin's Press); Penguin Group (Berkley, NAL), Random House (Ballantine-Bantam-Dell), (**Editorial Update:** now it's Penguin Random House. Merged!) and Simon & Schuster (Pocket, Gallery Books, Scribner). There's also Kensington and

Sourcebooks, which are independent but still huge NY publishers. And Harlequin, of course. So, there's more than six, but when publishing peeps are talking about the Big 6 (**or Big 5, in 2014**), you know they're talking about these guys and not, say, a small e-pub.

Vanity publishing: when a company charges you a lot of money to sell you a pile of overpriced books that you then have to distribute yourself. Just. Say. No. One of my son's teachers fell for this, and I felt so bad for her. When she heard I was an author, she said, "Oh wow, I'm an author too!" I said "Great! What house are you with?" She shook her head. "No, no, I'm self-published." "That's great!" I said. "How are sales?" "Well," she said, "I've sold nine books to my family and friends. But once sales pick up, I'm going to hire my son to ship them for me to the readers." "Ship…the books?" I asked, confused. Confused because you can set up an account on CreateSpace and have them print your books POD style and they ship for you, and at a reasonable cost too. "Someday I'll make back the thousands I spent," she said wistfully. OMG. Please don't let this happen to you. Please.

***

Okay. Here is a perfect example of why I love Twitter. I'm writing this essay, wondering what else writers want to learn about. So I asked. Within minutes, I got back a whole slew of responses. Well, my darlings, ask and ye shall receive. Remember how I said that your query letter is uber-important? I'm going to include the query letter that got me my first agent, along with exactly why I wrote what I did. I know this is a good query because almost every single agent I sent it to requested pages, and I ended up landing the agent who went on to sell seven books on my behalf. I checked out their website, doing my research before going to a panel where this agent would be speaking. At the time, I thought, hmm. Somehow I doubt they're going to want little ol' me, an erotic romance author. But when I heard this agent speak, it was clear she was actively looking to build her romance list. And so, I queried with the following email. I'm going to put my own notes to you guys in ***bold italics*** so you can see why I wrote what I did.

***

Dear First Name Last Name: ***Spell the name right, use the whole name. This isn't time to be cutesy or unprofessional!***

It was great meeting you on Saturday at the NJ RWA agent/editor panel. I enjoyed chatting with you at lunch :) ***I remind her where we met, which helps make the query more personal.*** I have a manuscript I'm seeking representation for, if you're interested in seeing it I'd be happy to email you a copy (and I'll make sure it's *not* in Courier New). ***This is a joke, since she made a comment on the panel about hating to read in the Courier New font. I'm showing her I'm friendly and that I was listening. But when in doubt, don't joke, because it won't always*** *sound right.*

PROTECTING EMILY is a completed 76,000 word romance set in post-apocalyptic New York City. *I told her the name of the manuscript, the approximate computer word count, the genre, and that it's complete. FYI, it's been retitled THE PULSE.*

It's been one year since an electromagnetic pulse destroyed America's infrastructure and took down the power grid, throwing the country into a new Dark Age. *This first sentence is designed to draw her in and get her excited to hear about the book. Then I go into the blurb, which should sound a bit like back-cover copy.* Emily Rosen lives in a military camp at Grand Central Station, where women act as the soldiers' private harem, selling their bodies on the tracks for extra rations. Emily escapes Grand Central and goes on the run from the soldiers intent on killing her for the secret she's discovered—America is rebuilding outside of New York City, and everything the city's refugees have been told is a lie.

Christopher Mason, a convict who broke out of prison after the Pulse, finds Emily before the soldiers do. Mason's survived on the streets of New York City this long by looking out only for himself—but there's something about the beautiful young woman that makes her impossible to leave behind. Now Emily must convince this intimidating, magnetic stranger to be her protector and guide as they journey out of New York and into the unknown. For Mason's protection, Emily barters the only thing anyone's valued since the Pulse—her body. But sex with Mason can never be just currency—it's pure passion, and everything she desires. *I spent weeks perfecting that pitch, LOL*

This is the first book in a potential series. *Notice I'm not trying to pitch more than one book at a time to her. I just mention that it could be a series. Sure enough, after I signed with her, she requested a synopsis of the entire Pulse Trilogy.*

I write erotic romance under the pen name Shoshanna Evers. PUNISHING THE ART THIEF, GINGER SNAP, and HOLLYWOOD SPANK are available now from Ellora's Cave (published late 2010 and early 2011); CHASTITY BELT releases April 20th with Ellora's Cave. TASTE OF CANDY will be published this year by The Wild Rose Press. "The Wooden Pony", an erotic short story, will be published in December 2011 in the Berkley Heat anthology AGONY/ECSTASY. *Here I listed my publishing credits. I'm happy to say that I can now add about another ten books and anthologies with a dozen more on the way. Yeah, I've been busy.*

I'm an active member of RWA and my local chapter. At Romanticon 2010, Ellora's Cave presented me with an award for "2010 Rising Star".

Thank you for your time and consideration. I'm glad we got a chance to meet in person :)

Sincerely,

Shoshanna Evers ***And that's it. I ended it by thanking her, and closed professionally.***

***

(**Editorial update:** Did you like my pitch for The Pulse (http://shoshannaevers.com/post-apocalyptic-dystopian/)? It's been released as a Simon & Schuster Pocket Star trilogy in 2013 and 2014!)

So that's my winning query letter. She requested the full manuscript the following day. A few weeks later, she sent me a message on Twitter, saying "I'm loving this mss. Back to you ASAP."

Then, I had a chance to meet her again a few weeks later at BEA (Book Expo America) in NYC. I was there doing a signing at the Ellora's Cave booth, and the agent came over and invited me to lunch, where she offered me representation. Whee! I've been wanting an agent since I wrote my first novel at the age of nineteen. Of course, my first book was terrible, but I didn't know that.

But wait! I hear you say. That's not fair, you were already multi-published, you already met her in person, etc etc. Please believe me when I say that ultimately, while that probably peaked her interest, it's always the book blurb that sells the query. If a manuscript is amazing, agents and editors don't care if you've never been published before.

So tweak that blurb till it shines like the top of the Chrysler Building. Yes, I know Miss Hannigan said something like that in "Annie". That's okay.

2014 Agent Update: I recently separated amicably from my agent after three years and seven books sold. It happens. Some authors are blessed to have one agent be the perfect fit for each stage of their career, and sometimes authors need to move forward. So if you find yourself needing something more from an agency, don't get too depressed over it— it's not the end of the world!

There's a few more tidbits of advice I'd like to pass on, in no particular order. Format your manuscript using 1 inch margins all around, double spaced Times New Roman or Courier New 12 point font, put your name and the book's title in the upper left of the page header, and the page number in the upper right corner, with no period after. Use your paragraph formatting to create 0.5 inch first line indents (never tabs! Never never. Tabs mess up formatting when the document is emailed to the agent or editor's Kindle, which it will be).

If you decide to self-publish, get a slew of beta-readers, preferably other writers you've met online who won't be afraid to rip your manuscript's guts out. Trust me when I say you'd much rather hear how awful your book is in the privacy of your inbox rather than splashed across your Amazon product page with one star reviews.

If you decide to go the traditional route and get an agent, steel yourself for rejection. I've gotten so many rejection letters over the years I've stopped counting. But guess what? If I quit after the first (or second, or third, or...um, you get the idea) rejection, I wouldn't have become a successful author. Recently I read a self-published book called GO FOR NO by Richard Fenton & Andrea Waltz that I absolutely adored. The concept is to set a "no" quota for yourself. Tell yourself you won't rest until you collect a certain amount of rejection letters that year. I've heard of people finding their agent on the 146th try. And we all know that J.K. Rowling was rejected all over the place before she became a bestselling billionaire. What if she had given up after the tenth rejection letter?

I hope this book has been helpful to you— that the tips and advice you've gleaned from these essays will help you become a successfully self-published author. If you liked this book, I speak on behalf of all of the contributors when I say we'd really love if you'd consider leaving a review on Amazon and Barnes & Noble, or wherever you bought the book. Tell your friends.

Remember we're all in this together—there's no such thing as too many wonderful authors or too many fabulous books to read. The world is big enough for us all, which is why I created this book. Now seriously, get to work—I want to read *your* future book!

Happy writing!

19
HELPFUL LINKS AND RESOURCES

How to upload your book to Amazon:
https://kdp.amazon.com/self-publishing/help/

Video tutorial on How to Publish on Amazon:
https://kdp.amazon.com/self-publishing/help?topicId=A2M7MM0UP7PHK0

How to upload your cover to Amazon:
https://kdp.amazon.com/self-publishing/help?topicId=A2J0TRG6OPX0VM

How to convert your manuscript into a formatted ebook:
https://www.createspace.com/en/community/community/resources/formatting_your_files?view=blog

Professional Conversion services to create your ebook files (links to a list)
https://kdp.amazon.com/self-publishing/help?topicId=A3RRQXI478DDG7

How to download a template for a print cover at Createspace:
https://www.createspace.com/Help/Book/Artwork.do

How to make your ebook a print book using Createspace:
https://www.createspace.com/

How to upload your cover image (300dpi) to Createspace for print:
https://www.createspace.com/Special/Help/Tools/CoverCreatorBooks.jsp

How to upload your book to Smashwords:
https://www.smashwords.com/about/how_to_publish_on_smashwords

Smashwords Style Guide Free Ebook (formatting for Smashwords):
http://www.smashwords.com/books/view/52

Smashwords Marketing Guide Free Ebook (how to promote your book)
http://www.smashwords.com/books/view/305

How to upload your book to Barnes & Noble Nook Press (for Nook):
https://www.nookpress.com/

The B&N Nook Press Help forum:
http://bookclubs.barnesandnoble.com/t5/NOOK-Press-Help-Board/bd-p/NOOKpress

Twitter 101: How should I get started using Twitter?
https://support.twitter.com/groups/31-twitter-basics/topics/104-welcome-to-twitter-support/articles/215585-twitter-101-how-should-i-get-started-using-twitter

Twitter Basics (lots of helpful links from Twitter.com)
https://support.twitter.com/groups/31-twitter-basics#topic_114

Create a Facebook Page for your Author Name and/or Book:
http://www.facebook.com/pages/create.php

A list of review sites that will review self-published books, from TheIndieView.com:
http://www.theindieview.com/indie-reviewers/

ABOUT THE AUTHOR

New York Times and *USA Today* Bestselling author Shoshanna Evers has written dozens of sexy stories, including The Man Who Holds the Whip (part of the bestselling MAKE ME anthology), Overheated, The Enslaved Trilogy, and The Pulse Trilogy (from Simon & Schuster Pocket Star).

Her work has been featured in Best Bondage Erotica 2012 and Best Bondage Erotica 2013, the Penguin/Berkley Heat anthology Agony/Ecstasy, and numerous erotic BDSM novellas including Chastity Belt and Punishing the Art Thief from Ellora's Cave Publishing.

The non-fiction anthology Shoshanna Evers edited and contributed to, How To Write Hot Sex: Tips from Multi-Published Erotic Romance Authors, is a #1 Bestseller in the Authorship, Erotica Writing Reference, and Romance Writing categories.

Shoshanna is also the cofounder of SelfPubBookCovers.com, the largest selection of one-of-a-kind, premade book covers in the world.

Shoshanna is a New York native who now lives with her family and two big dogs in Northern Idaho. She welcomes emails from readers and writers, and loves to interact on Twitter and Facebook.

Sexily *Evers* After...

Shoshanna Evers wants you to stay in touch!
Website: ShoshannaEvers.com
Newsletter (right side of the page!): ShoshannaEvers.com/blog
Blog: TheWritersChallenge.com
Twitter: Twitter.com/ShoshannaEvers
Facebook: Facebook.com/shoshanna.evers
Goodreads: goodreads.com/shoshannaevers
Email: shoshannaevers@gmail.com

******To my readers:** If you enjoyed this book, I'd love if you could leave an honest review! Reviews are so important, thank you for taking the time—I really appreciate it!

COPYRIGHT ACKNOWLEDGEMENTS

- Successful Self-Publishing: How We Do It (And How You Can Too!); The Introduction; and Getting Published: Copyright 2012, 2014 Shoshanna Evers.
- The Business of Publishing, an interview of Shoshanna Evers by author Cara Bristol: Copyright 2012 Shoshanna Evers and Cara Bristol.
- How I Make $20,000 or More a Month with my Self-Published Books: Copyright 2012 Kallypso Masters
- We Can: Copyright 2012 Gia Blue
- The Cover: Make it Professional!: Copyright 2012 H.P. Mallory
- I Did It My Way: Copyright 2012 Liz Matis
- Respect Your Readers: Copyright 2012 Katriena Knights
- 10, no *11* Successful Self-publishing Tips I Wish I'd Known: Copyright 2012 Heather Thurmeier
- A Dog, A New Genre, and a Charity: Copyright 2012 Jennifer Probst
- A Tale of Two Novellas: Copyright 2012 Skye Warren
- The Sky Is Not Falling, or Why 99-Cent Books (Probably) Won't Take Over the World: Copyright 2012 Jackie Barbosa
- Why I Love My Crazy Indie Life: Copyright 2012 Donna McDonald
- How I sold 17,000 books in four months: Copyright 2012 Debra Holland
- David Kazzie, Before & After: Copyright 2012 David Kazzie
- Twitter 101: Five Things about Twitter Authors Should Know (and Five you Don't Know): Copyright 2012 Valerie Bowman
- Marketing by the eBook Copyright: 2012 K. Rowe
- The World of a Steampunk Indie: Copyright 2012 Heather Hiestand/Anh Leod

CPSIA information can be obtained
at www.ICGtesting.com
Printed in the USA
BVOW08s0236061117
499647BV00001BA/94/P